Franz Schu
100 Song

MW00825055

Low Voice

Edited by Steven Stolen and Richard Walters

Assistant Editor: Mark Carlstein

Translations by Martha Gerhart
Music engraving by Thomas Schaller

On the cover: Leopold Kupelwieser, *Charade at Atzenbrugg*, watercolor, 1821, Museen der Stadt, Vienna. Schubert spent three summer holidays at an Atzenbrugg guesthouse managed by the uncle of his friend Franz von Schober, author of the poem "An die Musik." A group of arts-oriented friends customarily gathered there periodically for a few years. Schubert is seated at the piano in this depiction of a lively July evening of 1821. His friend and fellow musician Josef von Spaun is seated across from him, on the right side of the drawing. Schober has climbed the tree portrayed by the artist Kupelwieser. Another fellow musician, Johann Baptist Jenger, is framed in the doorway; friend Philipp Karl Hartmann is seated to Schubert's left.

ISBN 978-0-7935-4643-5

HAL•LEONARD®
CORPORATION
7777 W. BLUEMOUND RD. P.O. BOX 13819 MILWAUKEE, WI 53213

Visit Hal Leonard Online at
www.halleonard.com

Contents

Index of Poets

Preface

The talents of Franz Schubert (1797-1828) are well chronicled in any music history source. The high quality of his nine symphonies, choral pieces, and countless piano and chamber works make him, of course, a major European musical figure, particularly as a transitionary talent from the Classical to the Romantic. It is, however, his work as a song composer, producing some six hundred plus *Lieder*, which insures him a unique place in music history. Schubert, in fact, re-invented the *Lied*, going much further in the endeavor of setting poetry to music than anyone before him. His accomplishment, however great, could not have happened without the rise of German lyric poetry during his time and the final decades of the 18th century.

The life of Franz Schubert was not one of grand events and public achievements. He was first and foremost, and perhaps only, a musician. By the age of eighteen he had already written hundreds of songs, including "Gretchen am Spinnrade," which would redefine what a musical setting of a poem should be, and "Erlkönig," arguably the most famous *Lied* in the history of the genre. Schubert would, before his death, create a modern definition of the song cycle, with wondrous settings of mammoth groupings of poems by the little known Wilhelm Müller. In the miraculous last year of his life the composer created the greatest voice-piano-instrumental obbligato piece in the repertoire in "Der Hirt auf dem Felsen." His settings of poems by Rellstab and Heine were put together posthumously by a publisher to create, appropriately, Schubert's swan song, *Schwanengesang*.

Schubert's aesthetic success as a song composer speaks volumes about the public and private side of the man. Born in Vienna, and almost always happier in the city than in any other place, Schubert never found the public acclaim that most landmark talents seek. His greatness as a song composer and his understanding of intimate expression probably hindered his public image. Musical success at the time was measured against Beethoven in the concert hall and Rossini in the opera house. Schubert dreamed of triumph in both places, but never achieved it. Only one opera score was completed, *Alfonso und Estrella*, now mired in obscurity.

Schubert's art was more personal than theatrical, and that was true of his music-making. The circle of friends around the composer would gather in living rooms and parlors for evenings which came to be called Schubertiads. He's the only major figure in music history who spent his musical life almost exclusively in these small friendly gatherings; even the reclusive Chopin had a far more public life than Schubert. Schubert's personal devotion to his friends was paramount. In his quiet way, he had a strong impact on those he knew. More humble than some enormous talents, Schubert was open to the influences of his artist friends, among them Mayrhofer, Schober, Schwind, Spaun and Vogl. He lived and traveled with some of them; there is speculation that in the case of Schwind, there was even romantic involvement. The composer's intense loyalty to his friends even took him to jail briefly in 1822 when he was arrested with the politically active Bruchmann and Senn.

Though he never performed in public concert, Schubert played regularly in the weekly Schubertiads. That fact alone proves he must have been a competent pianist. He did, however, make allowances for his abilities. For instance, he altered the triplet figures in "Erlkönig" to duples to accommodate his pianistic limitations. These evenings would also include Schubert accompanying waltzes and improvising for the entertainment of the guests. He had many favorite singers, Johann Michael Vogl and Anna Milder Hauptmann among them. On occasion Schubert himself sang a new song for the intimate Schubertiad audience, though he never would have considered himself a singer, as described in his diary entry of June 13, 1816, "...I played Variations from Beethoven, and sang Goethe's 'Rastlose Liebe' and Schiller's 'Amalia.' Unanimous applause for the first, less for the second. I too felt that my rendering of 'Rastlose Liebe' was more successful than that of 'Amalia,' yet it cannot be denied that the essential musicality of Goethe's poetic genius was largely responsible for the applause."

As a composer Schubert was inspired by many. He loved the operas of Gluck, and discovered the baritone Vogl at a performance of *Iphegénie en Tauride.* Schubert also greatly admired Handel, and in his free time played through that composer's operas and oratorios. As for Beethoven, Schubert held him in high regard. Though they both lived in Vienna, the two never met until 1827, with Beethoven virtually on his deathbed. Schubert had dedicated a set of published piano variations to Beethoven in 1822. He brought the elder composer a copy, but finding him not at home, and humbled by the idea of a return visit, he simply left the new edition. Beethoven apparently approved of the set, and played them nearly every day with his nephew. Despite his enthusiasm for Beethoven, he preferred Mozart's *Don Giovanni* to *Fidelio*, and rated the overture to *Die Zauberflöte* higher than the *Fidelio* overtures.

The flowering of lyric Germanic poetry of the age with poets such as Goethe, Heine, Rellstab and Schiller, along with the contributions of Mayrhofer, Seidl, Hölty and Rückert, was, without a doubt, Schubert's greatest inspiration. Schubert easily understood poets such as Mayrhofer, Bruchmann and Senn as he regularly drank and dined with them. Schubert heard the lyric possibilities of poetry like no other composer before him. Goethe's poetry, in particular, is a large presence in Schubert's Lieder, totalling 74 songs. Schubert's versatility in re-creating strophic and through-composed forms relates directly to the highest quality of Goethe's work. Schubert earnestly sought validation and recognition from Goethe, contacting him in 1816 with song manuscripts for a proposed publication, only to have the songs returned without acknowledgement. In 1825 Schubert tried again, sending the poet the songs from Opus 19, asking permission to make the dedication on the score to the author. Goethe made a diary entry noting the arrival of the manuscript, but did not respond to the composer.

Franz Schubert lived a quiet, often lonely and tragic life. He was barely five feet tall, and affectionately, if not attractively, nicknamed Schwammerl ("Little Mushroom") by his friends. Money eluded him, and he spent many fruitless hours asking music publishers for more of it, though they were reluctant to invest in the work of a man known by so few. But perhaps the outward appearance of his life is misleading. Perhaps someone with a profound talent so rare finds happiness in his own private way when at the piano or when composing, something we can only guess at when listening to the best of his heaven-sent melodies.

Abendstern

poem by Johann Baptist Mayrhofer

D 806. Original key: A minor. This song was composed in March, 1824, and first published in 1833, in Book 22 of *Nachlass*. [*Franz Schuberts Nachgelassene musikalische Dichtungen für Gesang und Pianoforte*; published in 50 volumes, in 1830, by A. Diabelli of Vienna] The poem comes from Mayrhofer's first published collection of poetry, dated 1824. The song is part of three settings (D 805–7) of Mayrhofer poems which Schubert wrote during the deterioration of their friendship. Mayrhofer (1787–1836) met Schubert through Josef von Spaun in 1814. Schubert left home in 1816, was strongly influenced by the poet, and shared a room with him for many years. Mayrhofer was affected dramatically by Schubert's death, and wrote very little after that event, finally committing suicide in 1836.

Abendstern	*Evening Star*
Was weilst du einsam an dem Himmel,	*Why stay you alone in the heaven,*
O schöner Stern? und bist so mild;	*oh beautiful star? And you are so gentle—*
Warum entfernt das funkelnde Gewimmel	*why distances the sparkling multitude*
Der Brüder sich von deinem Bild?	*of brothers from your visage?*
»Ich bin der Liebe treuer Stern,	*"I am the true star of love;*
Sie halten sich von Liebe fern.«	*they keep themselves distant from love."*
So solltest du zu ihnen gehen,	*Then you should go to them,*
Bist du der Liebe, zaudre nicht!	*if you are love; delay not!*
Wer möchte denn dir widerstehen?	*Who would want, then, to resist you?*
Du süßes, eigensinnig Licht.	*You sweet, headstrong light!*
»Ich säe, schaue keinen Keim,	*"I sow, behold no sprout,*
Und bleibe trauernd still daheim.«	*and remain, mourning silently, here."*

fernt das fun-keln-de Ge - wim - mel der Brü-der sich___ von dei-nem Bild?

»Ich bin der Lie - be treu - er Stern,___ sie hal-ten sich von Lie - be___

Etwas schneller

fern.« So soll-test du zu ih - nen ge - hen, bist du der

Lie - be, zau - dre nicht! Wer möch-te denn dir wi-der - ste - hen? du sü - ßes,

cresc.

ei - gen-sin-nig Licht. »Ich sä - e, schau - e kei - nen

pp

Keim,— und blei-be trau - ernd still_ da - heim.«

pp

Abschied

poem by Johann Baptist Mayrhofer

D 475. Original key. Schubert's title: "Abschied. Nach einer Wallfahrtsarie." [Parting. In the Manner of a Pilgrimage Aria.] The poem, in its original form, was entitled "Lunz," a village in Lower Austria. The song was composed in September of 1816, a time when Schubert was particularly interested in the poetry of Mayrhofer. A version of "Abschied" for solo piano, by J.P. Gotthart, was published in 1876. The first publication of the song as Schubert composed it, was in 1885, by Peters. See "Abendstern" for notes on Mayrhofer.

Abschied	Departure
Über die Berge	Over the mountains
Zieht ihr fort,	you go forth;
Kommt an manchen	you come to many a
Grünen Ort;	verdant spot.
Muss zurücke	I must return
Ganz allein,	all alone;
Lebet wohl!	farewell!
Es muss so sein.	It must be so.
Scheiden,	To part,
Meiden,	to flee
Was man liebt,	what one loves,
Ach wie wird	ah, how becomes
Das Herz betrübt!	the heart sorrowful!
O Seenspiegel,	Oh, reflecting lakes,
Wald und Hügel	forest and hill
Schwinden all;	all vanish;
Hör' verschwimmen	I hear, becoming faint,
Eurer Stimmen	your voices'
Wiederhall.	echo:
Lebt wohl!	"Farewell,"
Klingt klagevoll.	it rings, full of lament.

14

ach wie wird das— Herz be-trübt.

Schei-den, mei - den, was man liebt; Lebt

wohl! klingt kla - ge - voll.

Am Grabe Anselmos

poem by Matthias Claudius

D 504. Original key: E-flat minor. The poem's original title was "Bei dem Grabe Anselmos" [By the Grave of Anselmos]. That title also appeared on Schubert's first draft from November 4, 1816, and published in August, 1821 as Opus 6, No. 3 by Cappi and Diabelli, with a dedication to baritone Johann Michael Vogl. The title, "Am Grabe Anselmos" is found on a copy from an album of songs belonging to Theresa Grob, known to be the great love of Schubert's early years. This romantic interest began in 1814, when Grob sang the soprano solos in the first performance of his *Mass in F, D 105*. The Grob album was given as a birthday present to her in November, 1816, and consisted of seventeen songs, all in manuscript. Claudius (1740–1815) was a theology student, who later turned to political science and law before becoming a poet (using the pseudonym *Asmus*) and the editor of the *Wandsbecker Bote* [Wandsbeck Messenger]. In later life he became quite religious. See "Ganymed" for notes on Vogl.

Am Grabe Anselmos	At Anselmo's Grave
Dass ich dich verloren habe,	*That I should have lost you,*
Dass du nicht mehr bist,	*that you are no more,*
Ach, dass hier in diesem Grabe	*ah, that here in this grave*
Mein Anselmo ist,	*my Anselmo is—*
Das ist mein Schmerz.	*that is my sorrow.*
Seht, wie liebten wir uns beide,	*See how we loved each other;*
Und so lang ich bin, kommt Freude	*and as long as I live, joy will come*
Niemals wieder in mein Herz.	*never again to my heart.*

hier in die-sem Gra - be mein An-sel - mo_ ist, das

ist____ mein Schmerz,_ mein Schmerz,____ das_ ist____ mein

Schmerz. Seht, wie lieb-ten wir uns bei - de, seht, wie

lieb-ten wir uns bei - de, und so lang ich bin, kommt Freu - de

nie-mals wie - der in mein Herz, kommt Freu-de nie-mals wie - der in mein

Herz. Dass ich dich ver-

lo - ren ha - be, dass du nicht mehr bist, ach, dass

hier in die-sem Gra - be mein An - sel - mo— ist, das

ist_____ mein Schmerz,— mein Schmerz,_____ das— ist_____ mein

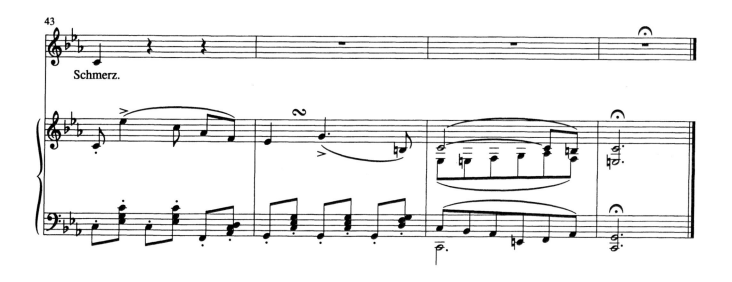

Schmerz.

Am See

poem by Franz Ritter von Bruchmann

D 746. Original key: E-flat major. There is some confusion regarding the date of composition of this song, with Kreisse's biography indicating it was written in March, 1817, but with no supporting evidence. Schubert was closest to Bruchmann in 1822–23, and there were two other Bruchmann songs written in the winter of that period. This song was published in April, 1831, in Book 9 of *Nachlass* (See "Abendstern"). Bruchmann (1798–1867), the son of a wealthy merchant, often hosted cultural events, including Schubertiades. A law student who became politically liberal, Bruchmann was arrested in March, 1820, along with poet Johann Senn and Schubert. After the breakup of the cultural and intellectual circle of influence, Bruchmann returned to the Catholic Church and became a Redemptorist priest.

Am See	By the Lake
In des Sees Wogenspiele	*Into the lake's play of waves*
Fallen durch den Sonnenschein	*fall, through the sunshine,*
Sterne, ach, gar viele, viele,	*stars—ah, so many, many,*
Flammend leuchtend stets hinein.	*flaming, glowing constantly therein.*
Wenn der Mensch zum See geworden,	*If man becomes as the lake,*
In der Seele Wogenspiele	*into the soul's play of waves*
Fallen aus des Himmels Pforten	*will fall from heaven's gates*
Sterne, ach, gar viele, viele.	*stars—ah, so many, many.*

Wenn der Mensch zum See_____ ge - wor - den, in der

See - le Wo - gen - spie - le fal - len aus des

Him - mels Pfor - ten Ster - ne, ach,___ gar vie - le, vie - le,

Am See

poem by Johann Baptist Mayrhofer

D 124. Original key: G minor. The poem was written in commemoration of Duke Leopold of Brunswick, who drowned while trying to save one of his subjects from a flood in 1785. Schubert composed "Am See" on December 7, 1814, his first song with a text by Mayrhofer. An earlier version of the song, published by Peters, included only two verses of Mayrhofer's poem and two by Max Kalbeck. See "Abendstern" for notes on Mayrhofer.

Am See

Sitz ich im Gras am glatten See,
Beschleicht die Seele süßes Weh,
Wie Aeolsharfen klingt mich an
Ein unnennbarer Zauberwahn.

Das Schilfrohr neiget seufzend sich,
Die Uferblumen grüßen mich,
Der Vogel klagt, die Lüfte wehn,
Vor Schmerzeslust möcht ich vergehn!

Wie mir das Leben kräftig quillt
Und sich in raschen Strömen spielt.
Wie's bald in trüben Massen gärt
Und bald zum Spiegel sich verklärt.

Bewusstsein meiner tiefsten Kraft
Ein Wonnemeer in mir erschafft.
Ich stürze kühn in seine Flut
Und ringe um das höchste Gut!

O Leben bist so himmlisch schön,
In deinen Tiefen, in deinen Höhn,
Dein freundlich Licht soll ich nicht sehn,
Den finstern Pfad des Orkus gehn?

Doch bist du mir das Höchste nicht,
Drum opfr' ich freudig dich der Pflicht!
Ein Strahlenbild schwebt mir voran,
Und mutig wag ich's Leben dran.

Das Strahlenbild ist oft betränt
Wenn es durch meinen Busen brennt:
Die Tränen weg vom Wangenrot,
Und dann in tausendfachen Tod!

Du warst so menschlich, warst so hold,
O großer deutscher Leopold!
Die Menschheit füllte dich so ganz
Und reichte dir den Opferkranz.

Und hehr geschmückt sprangst du hinab,
Für Menschen in das Wellengrab.
Vor dir erbleicht, o Fürstensohn,
Thermopylae und Marathon!

Das Schilfrohr neiget seufzend sich,
Die Uferblumen grüßen mich,
Der Vogel klagt, die Lüfte wehn,
Vor Schmerzeslust möcht' ich vergehn!

By the Lake

When I sit on the grass by the smooth lake,
over my soul steals sweet sorrow;
as from Aeolian harps stirs in me
an inexpressible magical fantasy.

The bulrushes bend down, sighing;
the flowers on the bank greet me;
the bird laments, the breezes blow—
from pain's pleasure would I perish!

How life gushes vigorously around me
and plays in rapid currents.
How it now ferments in cloudy mass
and now becomes bright as a mirror.

Consciousness of my utmost strength
creates a sea of joy in me.
I plunge bravely into its flood
and strive for the highest good.

Oh life, you are so heavenly beautiful
in your depths, at your heights.
Shall I not see your friendly light,
Hades' dark path to tread?

Yet are you not for me the ultimate;
as that, I joyfully sacrifice you to duty.
A shining image moves me onwards,
and bravely will I risk my life thereon.

The shining image is often moist with tears
when it through my bosom burns
the tears away from my red cheeks
and then dies a thousandfold death!

You were so humane, were so gracious,
oh great German Leopold!
Mankind trusted you so completely,
and presented to you the sacrificial wreath.

And, nobly adorned, you lept down
for men into the waves' grave.
Before you pale, oh son of princes,
Thermopylae and Marathon.

The bulrushes bend down, sighing;
the flowers on the bank greet me;
the bird laments, the breezes blow—
from pain's pleasure would I perish!

ich ver-gehn, vor— Schmer-zes-lust möcht ich ver-gehn!

Recitative

Wie mir das Le-ben kräf-tig quillt und sich in ra-schen Strö-men spielt.

Geschwind

Wie's bald in trü-ben Mas-sen gärt und bald zum Spie-gel sich ver-

klärt.

Be-wusst-sein mei - ner tiefs - ten Kraft ein Won-ne-meer in mir er -

schafft.

Ich stür - ze kühn in sei - ne Flut und rin - ge um das höchs - te Gut!

Du warst so mensch - lich, warst so hold, ___ o gro - ßer deut - scher Le - o - pold! Die Mensch - heit fühl - te dich so ganz und reich - te dir den Op - fer - kranz.

Recitative

Und hehr ge - schmückt sprangst du hin - ab, für Men - schen in das Wel - len - grab.

Vor dir er -

bleicht, o Fürs-ten-sohn, Ther - mo-py-lae und Ma-ra-thon!

Tempo primo

Das Schilf-rohr nei - get seuf - zend sich, die U - fer-blu - men

grü - ßen mich, der Vo - gel klagt, die Lüf - te wehn, vor Schmer-zes-lust möcht' ich ver-gehn, vor

Schmer-zes-lust möcht' ich ver-gehn!

An den Tod

poem by Christian Friedrich Daniel Schubart

D 518. Original key. The precise date of this song (thought to be 1817) is not known, as the autograph was lost. A long poem, 16 verses, Schubert originally set only the first two. Later he also set verses 14 and 16, but the early Peters edition includes only the original settings by Schubert. The publishing history is murky, with a copy in the third volume of Albert Stadler's song album, dated 1817, another appearance in 1824, in a supplement in *Allgemeine musikalische Zeitung*, and once again in 1824, as a separate publication. It was later included in Book 17 of Nachlass (See "Abendstern"). Schubart (1739–1791) was both poet and musician and founded the journal, *Die deutsche Chronik*, in Augsburg. His outspoken political beliefs, capped by a satirical attack on the Duke of Württemberg and his mistress, resulted in a ten year prison sentence. His poetry is primarily remembered for its use in Schubert's music.

An den Tod	To Death
Tod, du Schrecken der Natur,	*Death, you dread of nature,*
Immer rieselt deine Uhr,	*ever trickles your hourglass;*
Die geschwungne Sense blinkt,	*the brandished scythe flashes,*
Gras und Halm und Blume sinkt.	*grass and stalk and flower sink.*
Mähe nicht ohn' Unterschied	*Do not reap indiscriminately*
Dieses Blümchen, das erst blüht,	*this little flower, which just bloomed,*
Dieses Röschen erst halb rot,	*this little rose, just half red;*
Sei barmherzig, lieber Tod!	*be merciful, dear death!*
Tod! wann kommst du? meine Lust!	*Death, when will you come, my joy?*
Ziehst den Dolch aus meiner Brust,	*When draw the dagger from my breast,*
Streifst die Fessel von der Hand,	*strip the fetters from my hand?*
Ach, wann deckst du mich mit Sand.	*Ah, when will you cover me with sand?*
Komm, o Tod! wenn dir's gefällt,	*Come, oh death, if it pleases you;*
Hol Gefangne aus der Welt:	*take the prisoners away from the world.*
Komm, vollende meine Not,	*Come, bring an end to my misery;*
Sei barmherzig, lieber Tod!	*be merciful, dear death!*

The second verse was omitted from the first edition.

im - mer rie - selt dei - ne Uhr, die ge-
Ziehst den Dolch aus mei - ner Brust,

schwung - ne Sen - se blinkt,_____ Gras und
Fes - sel von der Hand,_____ ach, und wann

cresc.

ff

Halm und Blu - me sinkt.
deckst du mich mit Sand.

Mä - he nicht ohn' Un - ter-schied die - ses Blüm - chen, das_ erst blüht,
Komm, o Tod! wenn dir's_ ge - fällt, Hol Ge - fang - ne aus_ der Welt:

mf

cresc.

15
die - ses Rös - chen erst — halb rot,   sei   barm - her - zig,
komm, voll - en - de mei - ne Not,   sei   barm - her - zig,

17
lie - ber   Tod,   sei   barm -
lie - ber   Tod,   sei   barm -

20
her - zig,   lie - ber — Tod!
her - zig,   lie - ber — Tod!

23

An den Mond

poem by Johann Wolfgang von Goethe

D 259. Original key: E-flat major. The original version of the poem was a love verse written to Charlotte von Stein in 1777–78. In 1786, the two separated and Charlotte revised the poem to express her unhappiness. Goethe used some of her version in the revision. Schubert wrote this as one of five songs to Goethe poems, on August 19, 1815. It was first published in Book 47 of *Nachlass* (See "Abendstern") in 1850. Goethe (1749–1832) is generally considered to be the greatest of German poets and certainly one of the most brilliant and influential minds in history. His vast output (133 volumes in the Weimar Edition) encompasses poems, novels, plays, scientific studies (running to 14 volumes), a famous correspondence with Schiller, and his magnum opus, the 12,000 line *Faust*, written over a period of some sixty years. Though Schubert never received the slightest approval or even acknowledgment from Goethe, he set more than seventy of his poems to music. Also see "Gretchen am Spinnrade." The complete poem has been reproduced here. Schubert set only the first four stanzas.

An den Mond	To the Moon
Füllest wieder Busch und Tal	*Again you fill bush and valley*
Still mit Nebelglanz,	*silently with misty radiance,*
Lösest endlich auch einmal	*and at last you release*
Meine Seele ganz;	*my soul completely.*
Breitest über mein Gefild	*You spread over my fields,*
Lindernd deinen Blick,	*soothingly, your gaze,*
Wie des Freundes Auge	*like a friend's eye*
Mild über mein Geschick.	*gently over my destiny.*
Jeden Nachklang fühlt mein Herz	*My heart feels every echo*
Froh und trüber Zeit,	*of happy and troubled times;*
Wandle zwischen Freud und Schmerz	*I alternate between joy and pain*
In der Einsamkeit.	*in solitude.*
Fließe, fließe, lieber Fluss!	*Flow on, flow on, dear river!*
Nimmer werd ich froh,	*Never shall I be happy;*
So verrauschte Scherz und Kuss	*so have flowed away laughter and kissing,*
Und die Treue so.	*and faithfullness so.*
Ich besaß es doch einmal,	*I possessed it once though,*
Was so köstlich ist!	*that which is so precious!*
Daß man doch zu seiner Qual	*That which, even in one's affliction,*
Nimmer es vergisst!	*never is forgotten!*
Rausche, Fluss, das Tal entlang,	*Murmur, river, through the valley,*
Ohne Rast und Ruh,	*without rest and without repose;*
Rausche, flüstre meinem Sang	*murmur, whisper melodies*
Melodien zu,	*to my song,*
Wenn du in der Winternacht	*when you, on winter nights,*
Wütend überschwillst,	*angrily overflow,*
Oder um die Frühlingspracht	*or swell around the springtime splendor*
Junger Knospen quillst.	*of young buds.*
Selig, wer sich vor der Welt	*Happy, he who shuts himself off from the world*
Ohne Hass verschließt,	*without hatred,*
Einen Freund am Busen hält	*holds a friend to his heart,*
Und mit dem genießt,	*and with him enjoys*
Was, von Menschen nicht gewusst,	*that which, not known by men,*
Oder nicht bedacht,	*or not thought about,*
Durch das Labyrinth der Brust	*through the labyrinth of the heart*
Wandelt in der Nacht.	*wanders by night.*

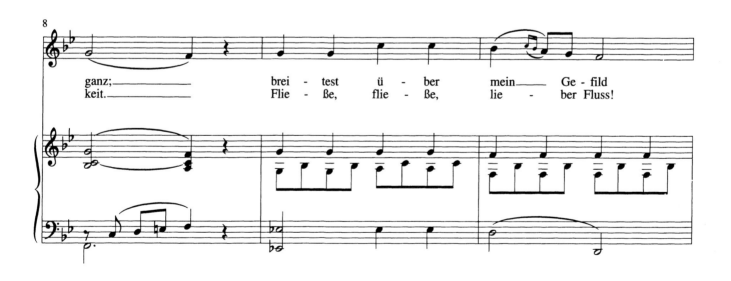

An den Mond

poem by Ludwig Christoph Heinrich Hölty

D 193. Original key: F minor. Composed on May 17, 1815, the original draft of this song did not include the piano prelude and it is assumed that Schubert added it when the song was published as Opus 57, No. 3, in April, 1826, by Weigel. "An den Mond" was the only Hölty song published during Schubert's lifetime. Its 12/8 meter and overall quality is remarkably like Beethoven's famed "Moonlight" Sonata. See "Seligkeit" for notes on Hölty.

An den Mond	To the Moon
Geuß, lieber Mond, geuß deine Silberflimmer	*Pour, dear moon, pour your silver glimmer*
Durch dieses Buchengrün,	*through this beechwood green,*
Wo Phantasien und Traumgestalten immer	*where fantasies and dream forms ever*
Vor mir vorüber fliehn.	*before me flee.*
Enthülle dich, dass ich die Stätte finde,	*Unveil yourself, that I may find the places*
Wo oft mein Mädchen saß,	*where often my maiden sat*
Und oft, im Wehn des Buchbaums und der Linde,	*and often, in the fluttering of the beeches and of the linden,*
Der goldnen Stadt vergaß.	*forgot the gilded city.*
Enthülle dich, dass ich des Strauchs mich freue,	*Unveil yourself, that I may delight in the shrubbery*
Der Kühlung ihr gerauscht,	*whose coolness rustled upon her,*
Und einen Kranz auf jeden Anger streue,	*and spread a garland on every mead*
Wo sie den Bach belauscht.	*where she listened to the brook.*
Dann, lieber Mond, dann nimm den Schleier wieder,	*Then, dear moon, then take your veil again,*
Und trau' um deinen Freund,	*and mourn for your friend;*
Und weine durch den Wolkenflor hernieder,	*and weep through the clouds' florescence downward,*
Wie dein Verlassner weint!	*as your forsaken one weeps!*

saß, und oft, im Wehn des Buch-baums und der Lin - de, der

gold - nen Stadt ver - gaß. Ent - hül - le dich, dass

ich des Strauchs mich freu - e, der Küh - lung ihr ge - rauscht, und

ei - nen Kranz auf je - den An - ger streu - e, wo sie den Bach be - lauscht.

An die Geliebte

poem by Josef Ludwig Stoll

D 303. Original key: G major. This song was written on October 15, 1815, the name day of Schubert's early love, Therese Grob. He finished seven other songs that same day. It was published by Peters, Leipzig, in 1887. Stoll (1778–1815), a Viennese journalist and publisher of the periodical *Prometheus*, was the poet for only two other Schubert songs. See "Am Grabe Anselmos" for notes on Grob.

An die Geliebte	To the Beloved
O, dass ich dir vom stillen Auge,	*Oh that I, from your silent eyes*
In seinem liebevollen Schein,	*with their loving shine,*
Die Träne von der Wange sauge,	*might lap the tears from your cheek,*
Eh' sie die Erde trinket ein!	*before the earth drinks them up!*
Wohl hält sie zögernd auf der Wange	*Well do they stay, hesitant, upon your cheek;*
Und will sich heiß der Treue weihn;	*it wishes to dedicate itself ardently to fidelity.*
Nun ich sie so im Kuss empfange,	*Now, as I receive it in my kiss,*
Nun sind auch deine Schmerzen mein.	*now are your sorrows also mine.*

die Trä - ne von der Wan - ge sau - ge, eh' sie die
nun ich sie so im Kuss emp - fan - ge, nun sind auch

Er - de trin - ket ein!
dei - ne Schmer - zen mein.

An die Laute

poem by Johann Friedrich Rochlitz

D 905. Original key. This is one of three Rochlitz songs written by Schubert in January, 1827, and published later that year on May 27, as Opus 81, by Haslinger. Rochlitz (1769–1842), a well known editor and the founder of *Allgemeine musikalische Zeitung* in Leipzig, first met Schubert in 1822. "An die Laute," like all of Opus 81, is dedicated to Rochlitz, and while the composer and poet admired each other genuinely, it is believed that the hasty publication of the Rochlitz songs was due to the fame of the poet and the opportunity to capitalize on his good name.

An die Laute	To the Lute
Leiser, leiser, kleine Laute,	*Softer, softer, little lute,*
Flüstre, was ich dir vertraute,	*whisper what I confided to you*
Dort zu jenem Fenster hin!	*that way, to that window!*
Wie die Wellen sanfter Lüfte,	*Like the waves of gentle breezes,*
Mondenglanz und Blumendüfte,	*moonlight and flowers' fragrances,*
Send es der Gebieterin!	*send it to my mistress!*
Neidisch sind des Nachbars Söhne,	*Jealous are the neighbor's sons;*
Und im Fenster jener Schöne	*and in the window of that fair one*
Flimmert noch ein einsam Licht.	*flickers still a single light.*
Drum noch leiser, kleine Laute:	*Therefore still softer, little lute:*
Dich vernehme die Vertraute,	*may you be understood by my beloved,*
Nachbarn aber—Nachbarn nicht!	*but by the neighbors—not by the neighbors!*

dort zu je - nem Fens - ter hin!
flim - mert noch_ ein ein - sam Licht.

pp

Wie die Wel - len sanf - ter Lüf - te, Mon - den - glanz_ und Blu - men - düf - te,
Drum noch lei - ser, klei - ne Lau - te: dich ver - neh - me die Ver - trau - te,

send es der_ Ge - bie - te - rin, send es der_ Ge - bie - te - rin!
Nach - barn a - ber_ Nach - barn nicht, Nach - barn a - ber_. Nach - barn nicht!

An die Leier

poem by Franz Ritter von Bruchmann

D 737. Original key: E-flat major. The actual date of composition of this song is unknown. Schubert's only close association with Franz von Bruchmann was in late 1822 and early 1823, and for this reason it is believed that this song and the other Bruchmann settings were composed during that period. It was published with two other songs, "Im Haine" and "Willkommen und Abschied," as Opus 56, by A.W. Pennauer in July, 1826. Bruchmann's poem is a translation of verses by Anacreon, a 6th century lyric poet. Anacreon's poetry was imitated by many writers in the late eighteenth and early nineteenth centuries because of its emphasis on the pleasures of life, love and nature. It was Schubert's idea to have the song printed in both German and Italian. See "Am See" for notes on Bruchmann.

An die Leier	To the Lyre
Ich will von Atreus Söhnen,	*I want to sing of Atreus' sons,*
Von Kadmus will ich singen!	*of Cadmus!*
Doch meine Saiten tönen	*But my strings sound*
Nur Liebe im Erklingen.	*only love in their resounding.*
Ich tauschte um die Saiten,	*I changed the strings;*
Die Leier möcht ich tauschen,	*the lyre I should like to exchange!*
Alcidens Siegesschreiten	*On Hercules' triumphant steps*
Sollt' ihrer Macht entrauschen!	*should its power roar!*
Doch auch die Saiten tönen	*But still the strings sound*
Nur Liebe im Erklingen.	*only love in their resounding.*
So lebt denn wohl, Heroen,	*So farewell then, heroes!*
Denn meine Saiten tönen,	*For my strings sound,*
Statt Heldensang zu drohen,	*instead of threatening heroic song,*
Nur Liebe im Erklingen.	*only love in their resounding.*

ih - rer Macht ent - rau - schen!
ci - de gli tro - fe - i!

Doch auch die Sai - ten tö - nen nur Lie - be im Er-
Ma che? se ce - tra e cor - de ri - pe - ton sem-pre A-

klin - gen, doch auch die Sai - ten tö - nen nur Lie - be im Er-
mo - re! ma che? se ce - tra e cor - de ri - pe - ton, sì, A-

Langsamer

pp

dim.

pp   3   3   3   3   *simile*

fz   *fz*   *decresc.*

klin - gen. So lebt denn
mo - re! *Eb - ben,* *e -*

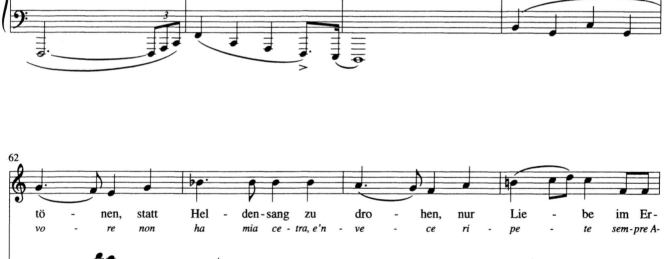

wohl, He - ro - en, denn mei - ne Sai - ten
roi, *ad - di - o!* *giac - chè per voi fa -*

tö - nen, statt Hel - den - sang zu dro - hen, nur Lie - be im Er -
vo - re non ha mia ce - tra, e'n - ve - ce ri - pe - te sem - pre A-

An die Musik

poem by Franz von Schober

D 547. Original key: D major. There are two version of this song, marked by different tempo indications. The original autograph, dated March, 1817, is marked *Etwas bewegt* [Somewhat agitated]. The other version, Opus 88, No. 4, (published by Weigl) is marked *Mäßig* [Moderate], with alterations in bar 5 (the addition of the grace note) and a changed bass line in bars 4 and 13. These changes might indicate Schubert's desire to revise the piece for publication. There is another copy, dated April 24, 1827, penned in an album for pianist Albert Sowinski. Schober (1796–1882) met Schubert in 1815 and was the poet for twelve of his songs. He studied law, but had many and varied interests, including poetry, painting, and lithography. He was for a time secretary to Franz Liszt. Schober was very close to Schubert throughout his life, offering him a place to live when Schubert left home in 1816 and for other short stints in 1822, 1826 and 1827–28. "An die Musik" was inexplicably excluded when Schober's collected poems were published in 1840 and 1855.

An die Musik

Du holde Kunst, in wieviel grauen Stunden,
Wo mich des Lebens wilder Kreis umstrickt,
Hast du mein Herz zu warmer Lieb entzunden,
Hast mich in eine bessre Welt entrückt.

Oft hat ein Seufzer, deiner Harf entflossen,
Ein süßer, heiliger Akkord von dir,
Den Himmel bessrer Zeiten mir erschlossen,
Du holde Kunst, ich danke dir dafür,
Du holde Kunst, ich danke dir.

To Music

You lovely art, in how many gloomy hours,
when life's fierce orbit entangled me,
have you kindled my heart to warmer love,
have you carried me away to a better world.

Often has a sigh, flown from your harp—
a sweet, holy chord from you—
unlocked for me the heaven of better times.
You lovely art, I thank you for this.
You lovely art, I thank you.

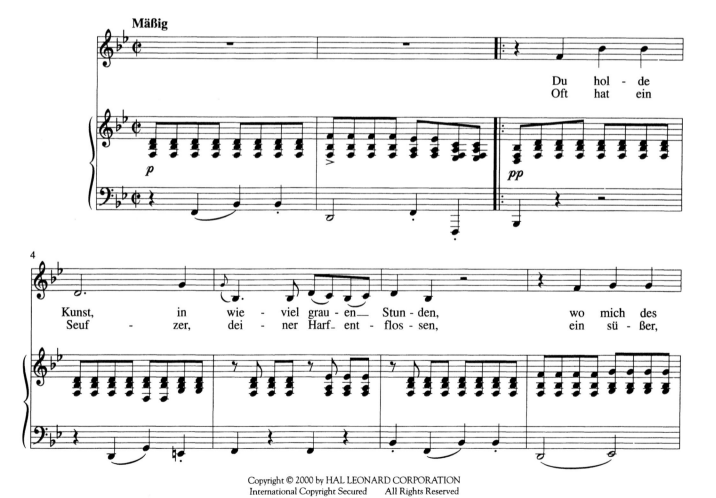

An die Nachtigall

poem by Matthias Claudius

D 497. Original key: G major. Claudius wrote his poem in 1771. Its original title was "Nachtigall, Nachtigall, ach!" The autograph of the song is missing, and the only evidence of a November, 1816 compostion date is an entry in the Witteczek-Spaun collection catalog. It was published by Diabelli in July, 1829, as Opus 98, No. 1. There is a striking comparison of the opening with that of "An die Geliebte," written just thirteen months earlier and possessing a nearly identical theme. See "Am Grabe Anselmos" for notes on Claudius.

An die Nachtigall	To the Nightingale
Er liegt und schläft an meinem Herzen,	*He lies and sleeps upon my heart;*
Mein guter Schutzgeist sang ihn ein;	*my good guardian spirit sang him to sleep.*
Und ich kann fröhlich sein und scherzen,	*And I can be joyful and can have fun—*
Kann jeder Blum und jedes Blatts mich freun.	*can delight in every flower and every leaf.*
Nachtigall, ach! Nachtigall, ach!	*Nightingale, ah! Nightingale, ah!*
Sing mir den Amor nicht wach!	*Do not sing my love awake!*

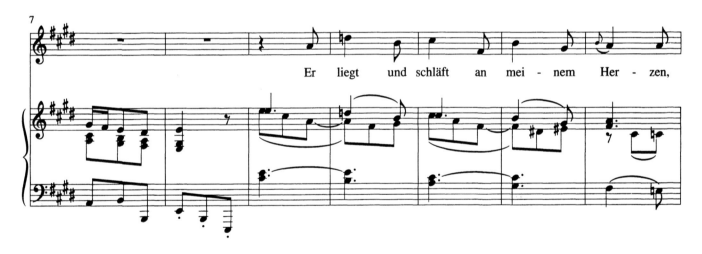

sang— ihn ein; und ich kann fröh - lich sein und

scher - zen, kann je - der— Blum— und je-des Blatts— mich— freun.—

Nach - ti-gall, ach! Nach - ti-gall, ach! sing mir den A -

- mor nicht wach!

An die Sonne

poem by Gabriele von Baumberg

D 270. Original key: E-flat major. Though the actual date of composition is unknown, it is believed that this song was written at the same time as four other Baumberg songs, in August of 1815. It was published in June of 1829, by Czerny, as Opus 118, No. 5. The original title of the poem, dated 1800, is "Als ich einen Freund des nächsten Morgens auf dem Lande zum Besuche erwartete" [As I awaited (seeing) a friend on the next day in the country on a visit]. Baumberg (1775–1839) was the wife of Hungarian political writer and poet, Johann Bacsanyi. The earliest known Schubert song (of which only an incomplete sketch exists) is set to a text of hers. He was thirteen at the time. Schubert set six of her poems in all.

An die Sonne	To the Sun
Sinke, liebe Sonne, sinke,	Sink, dear sun, sink!
Ende deinen trüben Lauf,	End your clouded course,
Und an deine Stelle winke	and in your place beckon
Bald den Mond herauf.	soon to the moon above.
Herrlicher und schöner dringe	More gloriously and more beautifully, urge
Aber morgen dann herfür,	tomorrow to come forth,
Liebe Sonn'! und mit dir bringe	dear sun! And with you, bring
Meinen Lieben mir.	my dear one to me.

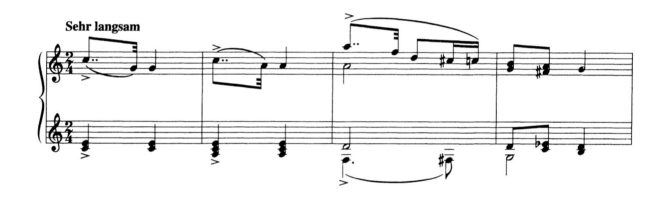

An die Entfernte

poem by Johann Wolfgang von Goethe

D 765. Original key: G major. Goethe's poem was written in 1788, and the subject is most certainly Charlotte von Stein, Goethe's love interest until their breakup at the time of the writing of this poem. "An die Entfernte" is one of four Goethe poems set by Schubert (D 764–767) in December, 1822, and published in 1868, by Wilhelm Müller in Berlin. See "An den Mond" for notes on Goethe.

An die Entfernte	*To the Distant One*
So hab' ich wirklich dich verloren?	*So have I really lost you?*
Bist du, o Schöne, mir entfloh'n?	*Have you, oh beautiful one, fled from me?*
Noch klingt in den gewohnten Ohren	*Still rings in my accustomed ears*
Ein jedes Wort, ein jeder Ton.	*each word, each sound.*
So wie des Wandrers Blick am Morgen	*Just as the traveller's gaze, in the morning,*
Vergebens in die Lüfte dringt,	*vainly into the atmosphere searches*
Wenn, in dem blauen Raum verborgen,	*when, in the blue expanse*
Hoch über ihm die Lerche singt:	*high above him, the lark sings:*
So dringet ängstlich hin und wieder	*So searches anxiously, from time to time*
Durch Feld und Busch und Wald mein Blick;	*through field and thicket and forest, my gaze.*
Dich rufen alle, alle meine Lieder,	*To you cry out all, all my songs;*
O komm, Geliebte, mir zurück.	*oh come, beloved one, back to me.*

floh'n? Noch klingt in den ge-wohn-ten Oh - ren ein je - des Wort,_ ein—

pp

Etwas langsamer

je - der Ton. So wie des Wand-rers Blick am Mor - gen ver-

pp

ge - bens in die Lüf - te dringt, wenn, in dem blau-en Raum ver-bor - gen, hoch

Geschwinder

ü - ber ihm die Ler-che singt: so drin - get ängst-lich hin und wie - der durch Feld und

cresc.

An Schwager Kronos

poem by Johann Wolfgang von Goethe

D 369. Original key: D minor. This song was originally published in 1825 as Opus 19, No. 1, by Diabelli, and bears a dedication to Goethe. It is believed to have been composed in 1816, a date based on the index of the Witteczek-Spaun collection, but there is no autograph of the composition. Goethe was 25 and traveling through the Alps in a post chaise when he wrote the poem. He based it on the word "Schwager," meaning "postilion, a rider of a team of two or four horses." See "An den Mond" for notes on Goethe.

An Schwager Kronos	To Coachman Chronos
Spute dich Kronos!	*Hurry, Chronos!*
Fort, den rasselnden Trott!	*Forward, at clattering trot!*
Bergab gleitet der Weg!	*Downhill glides the way!*
Ekles Schwindeln zögert	*Sickening dizziness comes over*
Mir vor die Stirne dein Zaudern.	*me at your dallying.*
Frisch, holpert es gleich,	*Quick, even if bumpy,*
Über Stock und Steine den Trott	*over sticks and stones with the trot*
Rasch ins Leben hinein!	*swiftly into life!*
Nun schon wieder	*Now once again*
Den eratmenden Schritt,	*the panting gait,*
Mühsam Berg hinauf!	*painstakingly up the mountain!*
Auf denn, nicht träge denn,	*Up then, don't be sluggish then,*
Strebend und hoffend hinan!	*striving and hoping upward!*
Weit, hoch, herrlich	*Vast, lofty, magnificent*
Rings den Blick ins Leben hinein,	*all around, the view into life;*
Vom Gebirg zum Gebirg	*from peak to peak*
Schwebet der ewige Geist,	*soars the eternal spirit,*
Ewigen Lebens ahndevoll.	*presaging eternal life.*
Seitwärts des Überdachs Schatten	*On one side a rooftop's shade*
Zieht dich an,	*attracts you,*
Und ein Frischung verheißender Blick	*and refreshment in the promising glance*
Auf der Schwelle des Mädchens da.	*of the maiden there on the threshold.*
Labe dich! Mir auch, Mädchen,	*Refresh yourself! For me too, maiden,*
Diesen schäumenden Trank,	*this foaming drink,*
Diesen frischen Gesundheitsblick!	*this fresh, healing glance!*
Ab denn, rascher hinab!	*Off then, faster downwards!*
Sieh, die Sonne sinkt!	*See, the sun is sinking!*
Eh sie sinkt, eh mich Greisen	*Before it sinks, before old age*
Ergreift im Moore Nebelduft,	*seizes me in the moor's mist,*
Entzahnte Kiefer schnattern	*toothless jaw chattering*
Und das schlotternde Gebein.	*and skeleton shaking.*
Trunken vom letzten Strahl	*Drunk with its last ray,*
Reiß mich, ein Feuermeer	*drag me, a sea of fire*
Mir im schäumenden Aug,	*foaming in my eyes,*
Mich geblendeten Taumelnden	*blinded, staggering,*
In der Hölle nächtliches Tor!	*to the dismal gate of hell!*
Töne, Schwager, ins Horn,	*Sound, coachman, your horn;*
Rassle den schallenden Trab,	*clatter at resounding trot,*
Dass der Orkus vernehme: wir kommen,	*so that Orcus may know we are coming,*
Dass gleich an der Tür	*so that right at the door*
Der Wirt uns freundlich empfange.	*the host may kindly receive us.*

neh - me: wir kom - men, dass gleich an der Tür_____ der

Wirt_____ uns freund - lich emp - fan - ge.

An Silvia

poem by William Shakespeare/Eduard von Bauernfeld

D 891. Original key: A major. Bauernfeld translated the Shakespeare verse from Act IV, Scene 2, of *The Two Gentlemen of Verona*. The song was published in early 1828 by the Lithographic Institute of Vienna, under the management of Franz von Schober, who held the manuscript copy. It was published again by Diabelli in 1829, as Opus 106. Schubert's autograph version was composed on handwritten staves in a small booklet which bears the inscription, "Währing, July 1826." Währing was a small village where the composer was spending a vacation with Schober. The song was dedicated to Marie Pachler, Schubert's patroness and hostess at Graz. Bauernfeld (1802–1890) was a Viennese poet, critic, and dramatist who, in 1826, wrote a libretto for Schubert's never-completed opera, *Graf von Gleichen*. His journals have provided us a wealth of information about Schubert and his closest friends in the composer's last years. See "An die Musik" for notes on Schober.

An Silvia	To Silvia
Was ist Silvia, saget an,	*What is Silvia, tell me,*
Dass sie die weite Flur preist?	*that the vast meadow commends her?*
Schön und zart seh ich sie nahn,	*Fair and fine I see her approaching;*
Auf Himmels Gunst und Spur weist,	*by heaven's favor and sign is directed*
Dass ihr alles untertan.	*that to her all be subject.*
Ist sie schön und gut dazu?	*Is she fair and kind as well?*
Reiz labt wie milde Kindheit,	*Her grace refreshes like gentle childhood.*
Ihrem Aug eilt Amor zu,	*To her eye hastens Cupid;*
Dort heilt er seine Blindheit	*there he cures his blindness*
Und verweilt in süßer Ruh.	*and lingers in sweet peace.*
Darum Silvia tön, o Sang,	*Therefore of Silvia resound, oh song,*
Der holden Silvia Ehren,	*to lovely Silvia's glory;*
Jeden Reiz besiegt sie lang,	*she has long won every grace*
Den Erde kann gewähren,	*which the earth can grant.*
Kränze ihr und Saitenklang.	*Garlands to her, and the sound of strings!*

Auf der Bruck

poem by Ernst Konrad Friedrich Schulze

D 853. Original key: A-flat major. It's believed this song was written in March, 1825, at the same time as "Im Walde." The songs were published together as Opus 90 (later changed to Opus 93) in May, 1828. While the Graz publisher, J.A. Kienreich, claimed the songs were written a year earlier, they were, in fact, two years old when Schubert made the publishing arrangements. Schulze (1789–1817) was engaged to the daughter of one of his Göttingen professors, but she died before they were married. His poetry depicts his bitterness toward the reality of his own life, which also ended tragically, due to tuberculosis, before he was 30 years old. There is some controversy as to the title of the song. "Auf der Bruck, den 25sten Julius 1815," is the poem's title as it appears in Schulze's *Poetisches Tagebuch* [Verse Journal]. "Bruck" is the name of a point on a hill near Göttingen. "Brücke," which means bridge, became part of the traditional, although not authentic, title for the song.

Auf der Bruck	On the Bridge
Frisch trabe sonder Ruh und Rast,	*Briskly trot without rest or repose,*
Mein gutes Ross, durch Nacht und Regen!	*my good horse, through night and rain!*
Was scheust du dich vor Busch und Ast	*Why do you hesitate at bush and bough*
Und strauchelst auf den wilden Wegen?	*and stumble on the rough paths?*
Dehnt auch der Wald sich tief und dicht,	*Though the wood stretches deep and dense,*
Doch muss er endlich sich erschließen,	*yet must it finally open up,*
Und freundlich wird ein fernes Licht	*and cheerfully will a distant light*
Uns aus dem dunkeln Tale grüßen.	*greet us from the dark valley.*
Wohl könnt' ich über Berg und Tal	*Well could I, over hill and vale,*
Auf deinem schlanken Rücken fliegen	*fly on your slender back*
Und mich am bunten Spiel der Welt,	*and the colorful pageant of the world,*
An holden Bildern mich vergnügen;	*the lovely images, enjoy.*
Manch Auge lacht mir traulich zu	*Many an eye smiles upon me comfortingly*
Und beut mir Frieden, Lieb und Freude,	*and offers me peace, love, and joy.*
Und dennoch eil ich ohne Ruh	*And yet I hasten without rest*
Zurück, zurück zu meinem Leide.	*back, back to my sorrow.*
Denn schon drei Tage war ich fern	*For the last three days have I been far*
Von ihr, die ewig mich gebunden,	*from her, who is eternally bound to me;*
Drei Tage waren Sonn und Stern	*for three days have sun and star*
Und Erd und Himmel mir verschwunden.	*and earth and heaven vanished for me.*
Von Lust und Leiden, die mein Herz	*Of pleasure and suffering, which beside her*
Bei ihr bald heilten, bald zerrissen,	*now healed, now broke my heart,*
Fühlt' ich drei Tage nur den Schmerz,	*I have felt for three days only the pain;*
Und ach, die Freude musst' ich missen.	*and alas, I had to forego the pleasure.*
Weit sehn wir über Land und See	*We watch the bird fly, over land and sea,*
Zur wärmern Flur den Vogel fliegen,	*to warmer meadows;*
Wie sollte denn die Liebe je	*how then should love ever*
In ihrem Pfade sich betrügen?	*be deceived on its path?*
Drum trabe mutig durch die Nacht,	*So, trot courageously through the night!*
Und schwinden auch die dunklen Bahnen,	*And though the dark tracks may disappear,*
Der Sehnsucht helles Auge wacht,	*the bright eye of longing is awake;*
Und sicher führt mich süßes Ahnen.	*and, safely, sweet presentiment guides me.*

ach,   die Freu - de musst' ich - mis - sen.

Weit sehn wir ü - ber

Land und See zur wär - mern Flur den_ Vo - gel_ flie - gen, wie

soll - te denn die Lie - be je in_ ih - rem Pfa - de_ sich be - trü -

Au - ge wacht, der Sehn - sucht hel - les Au - ge wacht, und

si - cher führt mich sü - ßes_ Ah - nen.

cresc.

f

p

f

p

Auf dem Wasser zu singen

poem by Friedrich Leopold Graf zu Stolberg-Stolberg

D 774. Original key: A-flat minor. The autograph for this song is lost, but it did appear as a supplement to the *Weiner Zeitschrift für Kunst, Literatur, Theater und Mode* in December, 1823. Two other copies also exist, one privately owned, the other transposed to A minor and now in the Witteczek-Spaun collection. It was first published in March of 1827 by Diabelli, as Opus 72, and is one of nine Stolberg poems set by Schubert. Stolberg (1750–1819) was influenced early by the poetry of Friedrich Gottlieb Klopstock (1724–1803), another poet much admired by Schubert. The poem was written in 1782, and titled "Lied auf dem Wasser zu singen. Für meine Agnes" [Song to Be Sung on the Water. For My Agnes]. Agnes was Stolberg's first wife and venerated as a true angel by their circle of friends and acquaintances. Following her death in 1789, Stolberg abandoned the more liberal views that marked his early years, and in 1800 he and his second wife became Roman Catholics.

Auf dem Wasser zu singen	*To Be Sung on the Water*
Mitten im Schimmer der spiegelnden Wellen	*Midst the shimmer of mirroring waves*
Gleitet, wie Schwäne, der wankende Kahn.	*glides, like swans, the rocking boat.*
Ach, auf der Freude sanft schimmernden Wellen	*Ah, on joy's softly shimmering waves*
Gleitet die Seele dahin wie der Kahn.	*glides the soul along, like the boat.*
Denn von dem Himmel herab auf die Wellen	*For from the heaven above, upon the waves*
Tanzet das Abendrot rund um den Kahn.	*dances the sunset round about the boat.*
Über den Wipfeln des westlichen Haines	*Above the treetops of the western grove*
Winket uns freundlich der rötliche Schein.	*beckons to us kindly the rosy glow.*
Unter den Zweigen des östlichen Haines	*Beneath the branches of the eastern grove*
Säuselt der Kalmus im rötlichen Schein.	*rustles the iris in the rosy glow.*
Freude des Himmels und Ruhe des Haines	*Joy of heaven, and peace of the grove*
Atmet die Seel im errötenden Schein.	*breathes the soul in the reddening glow.*
Ach, es entschwindet mit tauigem Flügel	*Alas, time vanishes on dewy wing*
Mir auf den wiegenden Wellen die Zeit.	*for me upon the lulling waves.*
Morgen entschwindet mit schimmerndem Flügel	*Tomorrow time will vanish with shimmering wing*
Wieder wie gestern und heute die Zeit,	*again, as yesterday and today,*
Bis ich auf höherem strahlenden Flügel	*until I upon loftier, more radiant wings*
Selber entschwinde der wechselnden Zeit.	*myself vanish in the flux of time.*

Mäßig geschwind

pp

simile

Mit - ten im Schim-mer der spie-geln-den_ Wel - len glei - tet, wie Schwä-ne, der
Ü - ber den Wip-feln des west - li - chen Hai - nes win - ket uns freund-lich der
Ach, es ent-schwin-det mit tau - i - gem_ Flü - gel mir auf den wie-gen-den

wan - ken - de_ Kahn.
röt - li - che_Schein.
Wel - len_ die_ Zeit.

Ach,_ auf_ der_ Freu - de sanft schim-mern-den_ Wel - len
Un - ter_ den_ Zwei - gen des öst - li - chen Hai - nes
Mor - gen_ ent-schwin-det mit schim-mern-dem_ Flü - gel

tan - zet das A - bend-rot rund um den Kahn, tan -
at - met die Seel im er - rö - ten-den Schein, at -
sel - ber ent-schwin - de der wech - seln-den Zeit, sel -

[*f*]

- zet das A - bend-rot rund um den Kahn.
- met die Seel im er - rö - ten-den Schein.
- ber ent - schwin - de der wech - seln-den Zeit.

f

[>] *p* [>]

fp

[ ]

1., 2.

3.

decresc.

Das Abendrot

poem by Alois Schreiber

D 627. Original key. This song was composed in November, 1818, and published by C.A. Spina in 1867, as Opus 173, No. 6, with the voice part, though written in the treble staff, marked, "Bass." Schubert was a tutor in the house of Johann Karl, Count Esterházy, and evidence suggests this song was written with him in mind. Schreiber (1763-1841) was a professor of literature at Heidelberg, drama critic and prolific author. Schubert set four of his poems, all in 1818. *Note: Some of the antiquated German spellings, such as the original's "Abendroth," have been modernized in this edition.*

Das Abendrot	The Sunset
Du heilig, glühend Abendrot!	*You hallowed, glowing sunset!*
Der Himmel will in Glanz zerrinnen;	*The heaven wishes to meld with radiance;*
So scheiden Märtyrer von hinnen	*so depart martrys from this life,*
Hold lächelnd in dem Liebestod.	*graciously smiling as they die for love.*
Des Aufgangs Berge still und grau,	*At dawn, mountains silent and grey,*
Am Grab des Tags die hellen Gluten,	*at the death of day, the bright embers;*
Der Schwan auf purpurroten Fluten,	*the swan upon crimson waters,*
Und jeder Halm im Silbertau!	*and every stalk in silvery dew!*
O Sonne, Gottesstrahl, du bist	*Oh sun, God's radiance, you are*
Nie herrlicher als im Entfliehn,	*never more glorious than in setting!*
Du willst uns gern hinüberziehn,	*You would gladly draw us toward*
Wo deines Glanzes Urquell ist.	*where the source of your splendor is.*

39

Halm im Sil - ber-tau; der Schwan auf pur-pur-ro-ten. Flu-ten, und je - der-

p   *p*   *cresc.*

42

Halm im Sil - ber-tau, und je - der Halm im Sil - ber-tau!

[*p*]   *pp*   *pp*

45

cresc.   *f*

Feurig, doch nicht zu geschwind

48

O Son - ne, Got - tes-strahl, du bist nie herr-li-cher als im Ent-fliehn!

f   *p*

Dass sie hier gewesen!

poem by Friedrich Rückert

D 775. Original key: C major. The Rückert poems Schubert set came from a collection of poetry called *Östliche Rosen* [Oriental Roses], and like the other Rückert settings, the composition date for this song is uncertain but believed to be late 1822 or early 1823. Originally untitled, this was one of the *Vier Gedichte von Rückert und Graf Platten* published by Sauer and Leinsdorf of Vienna in September, 1826. The title was added in 1830, when Diabelli reissued the opus. Rückert (1788–1866), the poet for six of Schubert's songs, was an academic with a particular interest in oriental languages and verse forms. He held teaching posts at both Erlangen and Berlin, but left academia in 1848 to pursue scholarship and authorship. Also see "Du bist die Ruh" and "Lachen und Weinen."

Dass sie hier gewesen!	*That She Has Been Here!*
Dass der Ostwind Düfte	*That the east wind's fragrance*
Hauchet in die Lüfte,	*breathes into the air—*
Dadurch tut er kund,	*thereby it makes it known*
Dass du hier gewesen.	*that you have been here.*
Dass hier Tränen rinnen,	*That here tears are flowing—*
Dadurch wirst du innen,	*thereby will you know within,*
Wär's dir sonst nicht kund,	*though it were otherwise not known to you,*
Dass ich hier gewesen.	*that I have been here.*
Schönheit oder Liebe,	*Beauty or love:*
Ob versteckt sie bliebe?	*Can they remain hidden?*
Düfte tun es und	*Fragrances and*
Tränen kund,	*tears make it known*
Dass sie hier gewesen.	*that she has been here.*

Der Jüngling an der Quelle

poem by Johann Gaudenz von Salis-Seewis

D 300. Original key: A major. Though all the other Salis settings come from 1815–16, no autograph of this song exists, so precise dating is open to conjecture. One of the two copies in the Witteczek-Spaun collection in Vienna is clearly dated 1821, so it could have been written at that time and not with the others. The song was published in Book 36 of *Nachlass* (See "Abendstern") in 1842. The original closing line of the poem was altered by Schubert from "Elisa! mir zu" [Elisa, come to me!] to "Luise, dir nach." [Louise, for you.] The *Gesamtausgabe* edition of the song restored the original "mir zu." This was the last of thirteen Salis poems set by Schubert. Salis (1762–1834) was an officer in the Swiss Guard in Paris prior to the revolution. He lived in Paris during the revolution and later returned to Switzerland to become an administrator.

Der Jüngling an Der Quelle

Leise, rieselnder Quell, ihr wallenden, flispernden Pappeln,
Euer Schlummergeräusch wecket die Liebe nur auf.
Linderung sucht' ich bei euch, und sie zu vergessen, die Spröde;
Ach, und Blätter und Bach seufzen: Luise! mir zu.

The Youth at the Spring

Gentle, trickling spring…you swaying, whispering poplars,
your slumber's stirring awakens only love.
Consolation sought I at your side, and to forget her, the coy one;
alas, and leaves and brook sigh: "Louise, come to me."

auf. _____ Lin - de-rung sucht' ich bei

euch, und sie zu ver - ges - sen, die Sprö - de; ach, und

Blät - ter und Bach seuf - zen: Lu - i - se! mir zu, ach, ___ und

Blät - ter und Bach seuf - zen: Lu - i - se! mir

zu. Lu - i - se! Lu -

i - se!

Der König in Thule

poem by Johann Wolfgang von Goethe

D 367. Original key: D minor. Gretchen sings this song after her first meeting with Faust, from *Faust*, Part I, Scene 8. The song was written for a collection of Goethe songs sent to Weimar in April, 1816, and was probably written earlier that year. It was published with four other Goethe songs as Opus 5, No. 5 in July, 1821, by Cappi and Diabelli, with a dedication by Schubert to his former teacher, Anton Salieri. See "An den Mond" for notes on Goethe.

Der König in Thule

Es war ein König in Thule,
Gar treu bis an das Grab,
Dem sterbend seine Buhle
Einen goldnen Becher gab.

Es ging ihm nichts darüber,
Er leert' ihn jeden Schmaus,
Die Augen gingen ihm über,
So oft er trank daraus.

Und als er kam zu sterben,
Zählt' er seine Städt' im Reich,
Gönnt' alles seinen Erben,
Den Becher nicht zugleich.

Er saß beim Königsmahle,
Die Ritter um ihn her,
Auf hohem Vätersaale,
Dort auf dem Schloss am Meer.

Dort stand der alte Zecher,
Trank letzte Lebensglut,
Und warf den heil'gen Becher
Hinunter in die Flut.

Er sah ihn stürzen, trinken
Und sinken tief ins Meer,
Die Augen täten ihm sinken,
Trank nie einen Tropfen mehr.

The King of Thule

There was a king of Thule,
utterly constant until the grave,
to whom his dying mistress
a golden goblet gave.

To him nothing was more precious.
He drained it at every feast;
his eyes filled with tears
as often as he drank from it.

And when he came near dying,
he counted up his towns in the kingdom;
he granted everything to his heirs,
the goblet excepted.

He sat at the king's banquet,
the knights surrounding him,
in the lofty ancestral hall,
there in the castle by the sea.

There stood the old tippler,
drank the last glow of life,
and flung the hallowed goblet
down into the water's tide.

He saw it plunge, fill up,
and sink deep into the sea.
His eyes lowered;
he drank never a drop more.

an ___ das Grab, dem ster-bend sei-ne Buh-le ei-nen
Städt' ___ im Reich, gönnt' al-les sei-nen Er-ben, den ___
Le-bens-glut, und warf den heil'-gen Be-cher hin-

gold-nen Be-cher gab. Es ging ihm nichts dar-ü-ber,
Be-cher nicht ___ zu-gleich. Er saß beim Kö-nigs-mah-le,
un-ter in ___ die Flut. Er sah ihn stür-zen, trin-ken

er leert' ihn je-den ___ Schmaus, die Au-gen gin-gen ihm
die Rit-ter um ___ ihn her, auf ho-hem Vä-ter-
und sin-ken tief ___ ins ___ Meer, die Au-gen tä-ten ihm

ü-ber, so oft ___ er trank dar-aus.
saa-le, dort auf ___ dem Schloss am Meer.
sin-ken, trank nie ei-nen Trop-fen mehr.

Der Alpenjäger

poem by Johann Christoph Friedrich von Schiller

D 588. Original key: C major. There are two versions of this song. The first is dated October, 1817, and is in E-flat major. There is no opening music except for a single chord; the song is 34 bars in length. The other, a copy in C major, is now lost, but an incomplete version of it exists in the Witteczek-Spaun collection in Vienna, and has a concluding section that was not part of the E-flat version. "Der Alpenjäger," dedicated to a friend, Schnorr von Carolsfeld, and published by Cappi in February, 1825, as Opus 37, No. 2, was most likely engraved from a copy made up by Schubert just for the occasion. The Cappi version alters the C major version's concluding section, and possesses a four-bar introduction. See "Gruppe aus dem Tartarus" for notes on Schiller. Another song entitled "Der Alpenjäger" is a setting of a Mayrhofer poem.

Der Alpenjäger

Willst du nicht das Lämmlein hüten?
Lämmlein ist so fromm und sanft,
Nährt sich von des Grases Blüten
Spielend an des Baches Ranft.
»Mutter, Mutter, lass mich gehen,
Jagen nach des Berges Höhen,
Jagen nach des Berges Höhn.«

Willst du nicht die Herde locken
Mit des Hornes munterm Klang?
Lieblich tönt der Schall der Glocken
In des Waldes Lustgesang.
»Mutter, Mutter, lass mich gehen,
Schweifen auf den wilden Höhen,
Schweifen auf den wilden Höhn.«

Willst du nicht der Blümlein warten,
Die im Beete freundlich stehn?
Draußen ladet dich kein Garten,
Wild ist's auf den wilden Höhn.
»Laß die Blümlein, lass sie blühen,
Mutter, Mutter, lass mich ziehen,
Mutter, Mutter, lass mich ziehn.«

Und der Knabe ging zu jagen,
Und es treibt und reißt ihn fort,
Rastlos fort mit blindem Wagen
An des Berges finstern Ort.
Vor ihm her mit Windesschnelle
Flieht die zitternde Gazelle.

Auf der Felsen nackte Rippen
Klettert sie mit leichtem Schwung.
Durch den Riss geborstner Klippen
Trägt sie der gewagte Sprung.
Aber hinter ihr verwogen
Folgt er mit dem Todesbogen.

Jetzo auf den schroffen Zinken
Hängt sie, auf dem höchsten Grat,
Wo die Felsen jäh versinken,
Und verschwunden ist der Pfad.
Unter sich die steile Höhe,
Hinter sich des Feindes Nähe.

The Alpine Hunter

Will you not guard the little lamb?
The little lamb is so innocent and gentle;
it feeds on blossoms in the grass,
frolicking by the edge of the brook.
"Mother, Mother, let me go
to hunt on the mountains' heights,
to hunt on the mountains' heights!"

Will you not coax the herd
with the merry sound of your horn?
Sweet sounds the peal of the bells
in the forest's joyous song.
"Mother, Mother, let me go
to rove on the wild heights,
to rove on the wild heights!"

Will you not attend to the little flowers
which in their beds cheerfully stand?
Out there no garden invites you;
harsh is it on the wild heights.
"Leave the little flowers, let them bloom.
Mother, Mother, let me go,
Mother, Mother, let me go!"

And the lad went hunting,
and pushed on and forged ahead,
restlessly ahead, with blind daring,
to the mountain's obscure part.
Before him hither, with the speed of wind,
flees the trembling gazelle.

Upon the rock's bare face
she scrambles with nimble flight.
Over chasms' cracked crags
she leaps daringly.
But behind her, boldly,
he follows with the deadly bow.

Now upon the jagged spur
she clings, on the highest ridge,
where the cliffs drop precipitously,
and the path vanishes.
Beneath her the steep mountain,
behind her the nearness of the enemy.

Mit des Jammers stummen Blicken
Fleht sie zu dem harten Mann;
Fleht umsonst, denn loszudrücken,
Legt er schon den Bogen an.
Plötzlich aus der Felsenspalte
Tritt der Geist, der Bergesalte.

Und mit seinen Götterhänden
Schützt er das gequälte Tier.
»Musst du Tod und Jammer senden,«
Ruft er, »bis herauf zu mir.
Raum für Alle hat die Erde,
Was verfolgst du meine Herde?«

With mute looks of distress
she implores the cold-hearted man;
she implores in vain, for ready to shoot,
he is already aiming the bow.
Suddenly from out of the cliff's crevice
steps the spirit, the mountain sprite.

And with his godlike hands
he protects the tormented animal.
"Must you bring death and misery,"
he cries, "even up here to me?
The earth has room for all;
why do you persecute my herd?"

Drau - ßen — la - det dich — kein Gar - ten, wild — ist's auf — den wil - den Höhn.

Geschwind

»Laß die Blüm-lein, lass sie blü - hen, Mut-ter,

Mut - ter, lass mich zie - hen, Mut-ter, Mut - ter, lass mich ziehn.«

p

ffp[———] *p*[———]
rit.

Geschwind

Und der Kna - be ging— zu ja - gen, und— es treibt und reißt ihn fort, rast - los
Auf der Fel - sen nack - te Rip - pen klet - tert sie mit leich - tem Schwung. Durch den
Jet - zo auf den schrof - fen Zin - ken hängt sie, auf dem höchs - ten Grat, wo die

fort mit blin - dem Wa - gen an des Ber - ges fins - tern Ort. Vor ihm
Riss ge - borst - ner Klip - pen trägt sie der— ge - wag - te Sprung. A - ber
Fel - sen jäh ver - sin - ken, und ver - schwun - den ist der Pfad. Un - ter

her mit Win - des - schnel - le flieht die zit - ter - de Ga -
hin - ter ihr ver - wo - gen folgt er mit dem To - des -
sich die stei - le Hö - he, hin - ter sich des Fein - des

zel - le.
bo - gen.
Nä - he.

cresc.

f

Mit des Jam - mers stum - men Bli - cken fleht_ sie zu dem har - ten Mann; fleht um -

p

cresc.

fz

sonst, denn los - zu - drü - cken, legt er schon_ den Bo - gen an.

fz fz fz ff

Langsam

Plötz - lich aus der Fel - sen - spal - te tritt der Geist, der Ber - ges - al -

ff

p

Der Musensohn

poem by Johann Wolfgang von Goethe

D 764. Original key: G major. This is one of four Goethe songs (D 764-767) contained in a manuscript dated December, 1822. While the first version of the song is in A-flat major, the initial publication, from July 1828, was transposed to G major. The opus, dedicated to Josef von Franck, and mistakenly numbered 87, was changed by the publisher, M.J. Leidesdorf, to Opus 92, No. 1. See "An den Mond" for notes on Goethe.

Der Musensohn

Durch Feld und Wald zu schweifen,
Mein Liedchen wegzupfeifen,
So geht's von Ort zu Ort.
Und nach dem Takte reget
Und nach dem Maß beweget
Sich alles an mir fort.

Ich kann sie kaum erwarten,
Die erste Blum im Garten,
Die erste Blüt am Baum.
Sie grüßen meine Lieder,
Und kommt der Winter wieder,
Sing ich noch jenen Traum.

Ich sing ihn in der Weite,
Auf Eises Läng' und Breite,
Da blüht der Winter schön.
Auch diese Blüte schwindet,
Und neue Freude findet
Sich auf bebauten Höhn.

Denn wie ich bei der Linde
Das junge Völkchen finde,
Sogleich erreg ich sie.
Der stumpfe Bursche bläht sich,
Das steife Mädchen dreht sich
Nach meiner Melodie.

Ihr gebt den Sohlen Flügel
Und treibt durch Tal und Hügel
Den Liebling weit von Haus.
Ihr lieben, holden Musen,
Wann ruh ich ihr am Busen
Auch endlich wieder aus?

The Muses' Son

Through field and wood roaming,
whistling my little song,
so I go from place to place.
And in time to my beat
and in measure moves
everything past me.

I can hardly wait for them:
the first flower in the garden,
the first blossom on the tree.
They greet my songs;
and when winter comes again,
I still sing my former dream.

I sing it far and wide,
upon the length and breadth of the ice,
there blossoms winter beautifully!
This blossom also vanishes,
and new joy is found
on the tilled highlands.

Then as I, by the linden
find the young folk,
at once I inspire them.
The dull fellow puffs himself up,
the awkward girl whirls
to my tune.

You give my feet wings
and propel over valley and hill
your favorite one far from home.
You dear, gracious muses,
when shall I repose upon her breast
finally, again?

Ziemlich lebhaft

Durch Feld und Wald zu schwei - fen, mein Lied - chen weg - zu -

pfei - fen, so geht's von Ort zu Ort, so geht's von Ort_ zu Ort. Und

nach dem Tak - te re - get und nach dem Maß be - we - get sich al - les an_ mir

fort,_____ und nach dem Maß be - we - get sich al - les an mir fort.

Ich

kann sie kaum er - war - ten, die ers - te Blum im Gar - ten, die ers - te

Blüt am___ Baum.   Sie grü - ßen mei - ne Lie - der, und

kommt der Win- ter wie - der, sing ich noch je - nen— Traum, sing

ich— noch je - nen,— je - nen Traum. Ich

sing ihn in der Wei - te, auf Ei - ses Läng' und Brei - te, da

blüht der Win- ter schön, da blüht der Win- ter schön. Auch die - se Blü - te

schwin - det, und neu - e Freu - de fin - det sich auf be - bau - ten

Höhn, _____ und neu - e Freu - de fin - det sich auf be - bau - ten Höhn.

Denn

wie ich bei der Lin - de das jun - ge Völk - chen fin - de, so - gleich er -

reg ich___ sie.   Der stump - fe Bur - sche bläht sich, das

stei - fe Mäd - chen dreht sich nach mei - ner Me - lo - die, nach

mei - ner, mei - ner___ Me - lo - die.   Ihr

gebt den Soh - len Flü - gel und treibt durch Tal und Hü - gel den

Der Neugierige

poem by Wilhelm Müller

D 795, No. 6. Original key: B major. This is the sixth song of the cycle, *Die schöne Müllerin*. The poems Schubert used for this cycle and his other great song cycle, *Winterreise*, are from a collection of seventy-seven poems, published as *Gedichte aus den hinterlassenen Papieren eines reisenden Waldhornisten* [Poems from the Posthumous Papers of a Traveling Horn Player], and subtitled, "To be read in winter." They were inspired by a party game in which the players did a charade of sorts, making fun of the simple Biedermeier folk poetry. Each player was expected to write and speak his "part" in verse, and it is these verses of Müller's, compiled over a number of years, which formed the published collection. The autograph for the song cycle is missing and the composition dates are not specifically known, though a draft of one of the songs is dated October, 1823, and Franz von Hartmann describes the Müller lieder among the pieces performed by Vogl and Schubert on July 28, 1823. It is believed that the cycle was completed sometime in November, 1823. *Die schöne Müllerin* was published in five books as Opus 25, by Sauer and Leidesdorf, and dedicated to baritone Karl, Baron von Schönstein. Müller (1794–1827), a poet, publicist and journalist, would probably be forgotten had it not been for Schubert. Though both resided in Vienna at the same time, they never met. See "Ganymed" for notes on Vogl.

Der Neugierige	The Curious One
Ich frage keine Blume,	*I ask no flower;*
Ich frage keinen Stern,	*I ask no star.*
Sie können mir alle nicht sagen,	*None of them can tell me*
Was ich erführ so gern.	*what I would learn so gladly.*
Ich bin ja auch kein Gärtner,	*I am indeed no gardener;*
Die Sterne stehn zu hoch;	*the stars are too high up.*
Mein Bächlein will ich fragen,	*My brooklet will I ask*
Ob mich mein Herz belog.	*if my heart deceived me.*
O Bächlein meiner Liebe,	*Oh my dear brooklet,*
Wie bist du heut so stumm,	*how silent you are today.*
Will ja nur Eines wissen,	*I want to know just one thing,*
Ein Wörtchen um und um.	*one little word, over and over.*
Ja, heißt das eine Wörtchen,	*"Yes" is the one little word;*
Das andre heißet Nein,	*the other is "no."*
Die beiden Wörtchen schließen	*The two little words comprise*
Die ganze Welt mir ein.	*the whole world for me.*
O Bächlein meiner Liebe,	*Oh my dear brooklet,*
Was bist du wunderlich!	*how strange you are!*
Will's ja nicht weiter sagen,	*I will really not tell others:*
Sag, Bächlein, liebt sie mich?	*say, brooklet, does she love me?*

Blu - me, ich fra - ge kei - nen Stern,— sie kön - nen mir al - le nicht sa - gen, was

ich er - führ so gern. Ich bin ja auch kein Gärt - ner, die Ster - ne stehn zu

hoch;— mein Bäch - lein will ich fra - gen, ob— mich mein Herz be - log.

Sehr langsam

O Bäch — lein mei - ner Lie - be, wie

pp

25 bist du heut so stumm, will ja nur Ei - nes

28 wis - sen, ein Wört - chen um und um, ein

legato

31 Wört - chen um und um. Ja, heißt das ei - ne

34 Wört - chen, Das and - re hei - ßet Nein, die bei - den Wört - chen schlie - ßen die

cresc.

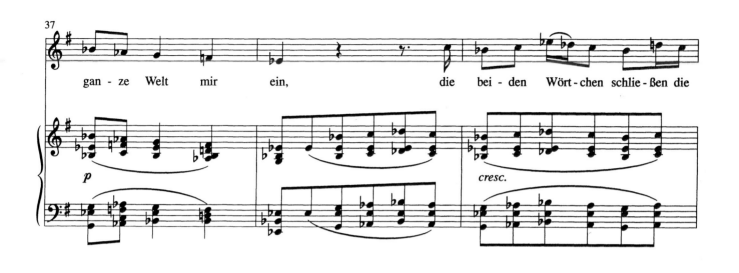

ganze Welt mir ein,   die bei-den Wört-chen schlie-ßen die

ganze Welt mir ein.   O

Bäch - lein mei - ner Lie - be,   was bist   du wun - der -

lich! Will's ja nicht wei - ter sa - gen, sag,

legato

Bäch - lein, liebt sie mich? sag, Bäch - lein, liebt sie

mich?

Der Tod und das Mädchen

poem by Matthias Claudius

D 531. Original key. This song was published in November, 1821, by Cappi and Diabelli as Opus 7, No. 3, with a dedication to Ludwig, Count Széchényi. Following Schubert's death, the autograph found its way to his step brother, Andreas, who divided it up into eight pieces, giving one to each of his favorite students. One of those pieces has the date February, 1817, believed to be the original composition date for the song. Sections of this song, notably the piano prelude and accompaniment figures, were adapted by Schubert in 1824 for the theme and variation movement of his D minor string quartet, D 810. See "Am Grabe Anselmos" for notes on Claudius.

Der Tod und das Mädchen	*Death and the Maiden*
Das Mädchen	*The Maiden*
Vorüber, ach vorüber,	*Pass by; ah, pass by.*
Geh wilder Knochenmann!	*Get away, wild skeleton!*
Ich bin noch jung, geh Lieber,	*I am still young. Away, dear man,*
Und rühre mich nicht an.	*and touch me not.*
Der Tod	*Death*
Gib deine Hand, du schön und zart Gebild,	*Yield your hand, you beautiful and tender creature;*
Bin Freund und komme nicht zu strafen.	*I am a friend, and come not to chastise.*
Sei gutes Muts! ich bin nicht wild,	*Be of good cheer! I am not wild;*
Sollst sanft in meinen Armen schlafen.	*you shall sleep softly in my arms.*

Freund und kom - me nicht zu____ stra - fen.

Sei gu - tes Muts! ich bin nicht wild, sollst

sanft in mei - nen Ar - men schla - fen.

Der Wanderer

poem by Georg Philipp Schmidt von Lübeck

D 489. Original key. Schmidt von Lübeck's literary fame is based totally on this one poem, published in 1808. The original title for the poem was "Des Fremdlings Abendlied" [The Stranger's Evening Song]. Schubert came across the poem with the title, "Der Unglückliche" [The Unhappy One], and changed it to "Der Wanderer." The autograph dates from October, 1816. A copy in Schubert's hand is transposed to B minor and written for bass voice. A third copy, published by Cappi and Diabelli in May, 1821, as Opus 4, No. 1, is in C-sharp minor, and is dedicated to the poet Johann Ladislaus Pyrker. "Der Wanderer" is the source for thematic material in Schubert's *Phantasie* in C major, D 760, for solo piano. Schmidt (1766–1849) studied both law and medicine. After practicing medicine he went into government service in Denmark. See "Die Allmacht" for notes on Pyrker. Another "Der Wanderer" by Schubert is a setting of a Schlegel poem.

Der Wanderer	The Wanderer
Ich komme vom Gebirge her,	*I come from the mountains;*
Es dampft das Tal, es braust das Meer.	*the valley is damp, the sea roars.*
Ich wandle still, bin wenig froh,	*I wander silently, am rarely happy;*
Und immer fragt der Seufzer: wo?	*and ever my sigh asks: where?*
Immer wo?	*Ever where?*
Die Sonne dünkt mich hier so kalt,	*The sun here seems to me so cold,*
Die Blüte welk, das Leben alt,	*the blossoms withered, life old,*
Und was sie reden, leerer Schall,	*and what people say, empty sound.*
Ich bin ein Fremdling überall.	*I am a stranger everywhere.*
Wo bist du, mein geliebtes Land?	*Where are you, my beloved land?*
Gesucht, geahnt und nie gekannt.	*Sought after, foreseen, and never known!*
Das Land so hoffnungsgrün,	*The land so verdant with hope,*
Das Land, wo meine Rosen blühn,	*the land where my roses bloom,*
Wo meine Freunde wandelnd gehn,	*where my friends go walking,*
Wo meine Toten auferstehn,	*where my dead ones are resurrected,*
Das Land, das meine Sprache spricht,	*the land that speaks my tongue…*
O Land, wo bist du?	*oh land, where are you?*
Ich wandle still, bin wenig froh,	*I wander silently, am rarely happy;*
Und immer fragt der Seufzer: wo?	*and ever my sigh asks: where?*
Immer wo?	*Ever where?*
Im Geisterhauch tönt's mir zurück:	*A ghostly whisper answers me:*
»Dort, wo du nicht bist, dort is das Glück.«	*"There, where you are not—there is happiness!"*

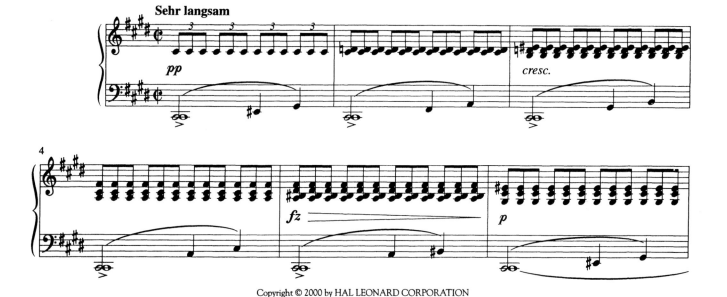

Ich kom-me vom Ge-bir - ge her,   es dampft das

Tal,   es braust   das Meer,   es

braust   das   Meer.

Ich wand-le___ still,   bin we - nig froh,

auf - er - stehn, das Land, das mei - ne Spra - che spricht, o Land,_____ wo

Tempo primo

bist du?   Ich   wand - le_____

still,   bin we - nig froh,   und im - mer

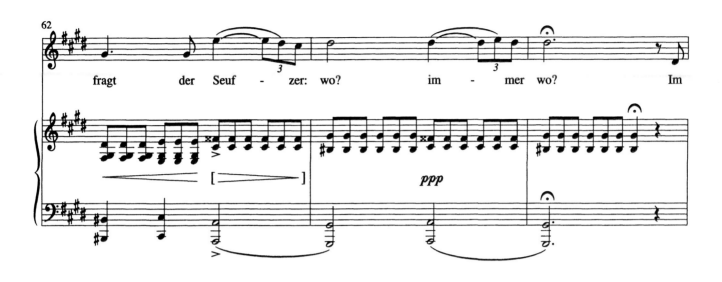

fragt   der   Seuf - zer: wo?   im - mer wo?   Im

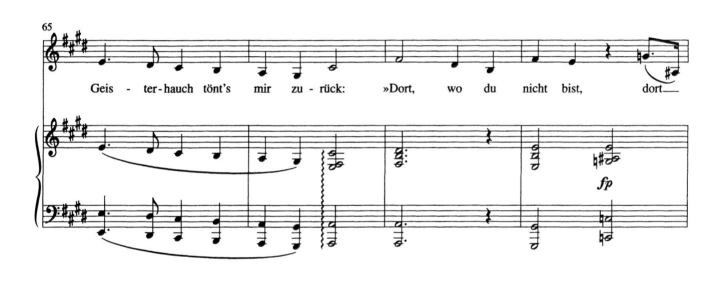

Geis - ter-hauch tönt's mir zu-rück: »Dort,   wo   du   nicht bist,   dort___

ist   das   Glück.«

Der Zwerg

poem by Matthäus von Collin

D 771. Original key. It's believed this song was written in November, 1822, based on the report that it was sung by Vogl at a party later that year. It was published as Opus 22, No. 1, by Sauer and Leidesdorf in May, 1823, with the present title, an alteration of the poem's original, "Treubruch" [Treachery], and dedicated to its author. Collin (1779–1824) was a professor of philosophy at Cracow and at Vienna. He also served as tutor to Napoleon's son, the Duke of Reichstadt, and was a cousin to Schubert's friend and supporter, Josef von Spaun. Schubert set five poems by Collin from 1822–23. See "Ganymed" for notes on Vogl.

Der Zwerg	The Dwarf
Im trüben Licht verschwinden schon die Berge,	In the dusky light the mountains are already fading;
Es schwebt das Schiff auf glatten Meereswogen,	the ship drifts upon the sea's smooth billows,
Worauf die Königin mit ihrem Zwerge.	on board the queen with her dwarf.
Sie schaut empor zum hochgewölbten Bogen,	She gazes upward at the lofty arch of the vault,
Hinauf zur lichtdurchwirkten blauen Ferne,	up into the blue distance interwoven with light,
Die mit der Milch des Himmels blass durchzogen.	faintly laced with the milky way.
Nie, nie habt ihr mir gelogen noch, ihr Sterne,	"Never, never yet have you lied to me, you stars,"
So ruft sie aus, bald werd' ich nun entschwinden,	she cries out. "Soon now I shall perish,
Ihr sagt es mir, doch sterb' ich wahrlich gerne.	you tell me; yet in truth I shall die gladly."
Da tritt der Zwerg zur Königin, mag binden	Then the dwarf steps to the queen, is able to tie
Um ihren Hals die Schnur von roter Seide	around her neck the cord of red silk,
Und weint, als wollt' er schnell vor Gram erblinden.	and weeps, as though he would quickly go blind from grief.
Er spricht: Du selbst bist schuld an diesem Leide,	He speaks: "You yourself are to blame for this suffering,
Weil um den König du mich hast verlassen,	because you have forsaken me for the king;
Jetzt weckt dein Sterben einzig mir noch Freude.	now your death alone will awaken joy in me again.
Zwar werd' ich ewiglich mich selber hassen,	To be sure, I will forever hate myself
Der dir mit dieser Hand den Tod gegeben,	for having brought death to you with this hand;
Doch musst zum frühen Grab du nun erblassen.	but you must grow pale now, to an early grave."
Sie legt die Hand auf's Herz voll jungem Leben,	She lays her hand on her heart, full of young life,
Und aus dem Aug die schweren Tränen rinnen,	and the heavy tears flow from her eyes,
Das sie zum Himmel betend will erheben.	which she would raise to heaven in prayer.
Mögst du nicht Schmerz durch meinen Tod gewinnen!	"May you not gain sorrow from my death!,"
Sie sagt's, da küsst der Zwerg die bleichen Wangen,	she says. Then the dwarf kisses the pale cheeks;
Drauf alsobald vergehen ihr die Sinnen.	thereupon, forthwith, she loses her senses.
Der Zwerg schaut an die Frau, vom Tod befangen,	The dwarf looks at the woman seized by death.
Er senkt sie tief ins Meer mit eignen Handen.	He sinks her deep in the sea with his own hands.
Ihm brennt nach ihr das Herz so voll Verlangen.	His heart burns so full of longing for her.
An keiner Küste wird er je mehr landen.	On no shore will he ever again land.

Sie schaut em-
por zum hoch-ge-wölb-ten Bo- gen, hin-auf zur
licht-durch-wirk-ten blau- en Fer- ne, die mit der Milch des Him-mels blass durch-
zo- gen. Nie, nie habt ihr mir ge-

jun - gem Le - ben, und aus dem Aug die

schwe - ren Trä - nen rin - nen, das sie zum Him - mel be - tend will er - he -

ben. Mögst du nicht Schmerz durch mei - nen Tod ge - win -

nen! sie sagt's, da küsst der Zwerg die blei - chen Wan - gen, drauf

al - so - bald_____ ver - ge - hen ihr die Sin - nen.

Der Zwerg schaut an die Frau, vom Tod be -

fan - gen, er senkt sie tief ins Meer mit eig - nen

Han - den. Ihm brennt nach ihr das Herz so voll Ver - lan -

gen, ihm brennt nach ihr das Herz so voll Ver - lan -

gen, so voll Ver - lan - gen.

An kei - ner Küs - te wird er

je mehr lan - den.

Die böse Farbe

poem by Wilhelm Müller

D 795, No. 17. Original key: B major. This is the seventeenth song of the cycle *Die schöne Müllerin*.
See "Der Neugierige" for notes on Müller and *Die schöne Müllerin*.

Die böse Farbe	The Hateful Color
Ich möchte ziehn in die Welt hinaus,	*I would like to go out into the world,*
Hinaus in die weite Welt,	*out into the wide world,*
Wenn's nur so grün, so grün nicht wär,	*if only it were not so green, so green*
Da draußen in Wald und Feld.	*out there in forest and field.*
Ich möchte die grünen Blätter all	*I would like to pluck all the green leaves*
Pflücken von jedem Zweig,	*off every branch;*
Ich möchte die grünen Gräser all	*I would like all the green grass*
Weinen ganz totenbleich.	*to turn, from my tears, deathly pale.*
Ach Grün, du böse Farbe du,	*Oh green, you hateful color you,*
Was siehst mich immer an,	*why do you always look at me*
So stolz, so keck, so schadenfroh,	*so proudly, so boldly, so gloatingly—*
Mich armen weißen Mann?	*at me, a poor miller?*
Ich möchte liegen vor ihrer Tür	*I would like to lie at her door*
In Sturm und Regen und Schnee,	*in storm and rain and snow*
Und singen ganz leise bei Tag und Nacht	*and sing very softly, day and night,*
Das eine Wörtchen Ade.	*the one little word "farewell."*
Horch, wenn im Wald ein Jagdhorn schallt,	*Hark! When in the wood a hunting horn resounds,*
Da klingt ihr Fensterlein,	*there's a sound at her window;*
Und schaut sie auch nach mir nicht aus,	*and although she doesn't look out to see me,*
Darf ich doch schauen hinein.	*I can yet look within.*
O binde von der Stirn dir ab	*Oh, untie from your brow*
Das grüne, grüne Band,	*the green, green ribbon;*
Ade, ade! und reiche mir	*farewell, farewell! And offer me*
Zum Abschied deine Hand.	*your hand in parting.*

Ich möch - te ziehn in die Welt hin - aus, hin - aus in die wei - te— Welt, wenn's

nur so grün, so grün nicht wär, da drau - ßen in Wald und Feld. Ich

möch - te die grü - nen— Blät - ter all pflü - cken von je - dem— Zweig, ich

möch - te die grü - nen— Grä - ser all wei - nen ganz to - ten - bleich,—

wei - nen ganz to - ten - bleich. Ach Grün, du bö - se Far - be du,

was siehst mich im - mer an, so stolz, so keck, so scha - den - froh, mich

ar - men, ar - men wei - ßen Mann? Ich

möch - te lie - gen vor ih - rer Tür in Sturm und Re - gen und Schnee, und

sin - gen ganz lei - se bei Tag und Nacht das ei - ne Wört - chen A - de, das

ei - ne Wört - chen A - de. Horch,

wenn im Wald ein Jagd - horn schallt, da klingt ihr Fens - ter - lein, und

schaut sie auch nach mir nicht aus, darf ich doch schau - en hin - ein. O

bin - de von der Stirn dir ab das grü - ne, grü - ne Band, das grü - ne, grü - ne Band, a -

de, a - de! und rei - che mir zum Ab - schied dei - ne

Hand, a - de, a - de! und rei - che mir zum

Ab - schied dei - ne Hand, zum Ab - schied dei - ne Hand.

f

Die Allmacht

poem by Johann Ladislaus Pyrker

D 852. Original key: C major. Written in August, 1825, this song was published by Haslinger along with another Pyrker setting as Opus 79, in May, 1827. The songs are dedicated to the poet. Pyrker and Schubert met during Schubert's visit to Bad Gastein in the early fall of 1825. The poem comes from *Perlen der heiligen Vorzeit* [Pearls from Holy Antiquity] and is one of the few Schubert songs based on a purely religious theme. There is some historical belief that the song was originally written for the great Schubertian baritone, Johann Michael Vogl, and if this is the case, it was probably written in A major and transposed to C major for the 1827 publication. Pyrker (1772–1847) was born in Hungary and ordained as a Catholic priest in 1796. In addition to his contributions as a poet to Schubert's songs, he also was a patron, and Schubert dedicated "Wandrers Nachtlied I," D 224, "Der Wanderer," D 493, and "Morgenlied," D 685, to him. See "Ganymed" for notes on Vogl.

Die Allmacht	*Omnipotence*
Groß ist Jehova, der Herr! denn Himmel und Erde verkünden	*Great is Jehovah, the Lord! For heaven and earth proclaim*
Seine Macht. Du hörst sie im brausenden Sturm, in des Waldstroms	*his might. You hear it in the raging storm, in the woods' river's*
Laut aufrauschendem Ruf, in des grünenden Waldes Gesäusel,	*loud roaring cry, in the greening wood's rustling;*
Siehst sie in wogender Saaten Gold, in lieblicher Blumen	*you see it in the waving corn's gold, in lovely flowers'*
Glühendem Schmelz, im Glanz des sternebesäeten Himmels.	*glowing effusion, in the splendor of the star-studded heaven.*
Furchtbar tönt sie im Donnergeroll und flammt in des Blitzes	*Frightful sounds it in the thunder's roll; and it blazes in the lightning's*
Schnell hinzuckendem Flug, doch kündet das pochende Herz dir	*rapidly flashing flight. Yet your throbbing heart will proclaim to you*
Fühlbarer noch Jehovas Macht, des ewigen Gottes,	*more clearly still the might of Jehovah, the eternal God,*
Blickst du flehend empor und hoffst auf Huld und Erbarmen.	*if you look up to heaven in supplication, and hope for grace and mercy.*

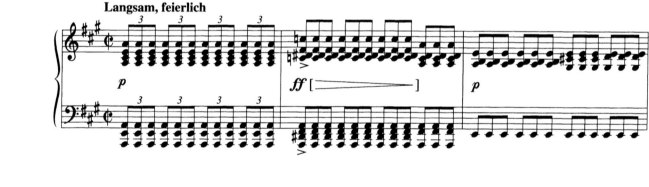

Die Forelle

poem by Christian Friedrich Daniel Schubart

D 550. Original key: D-flat major. The oldest of the five versions of "Die Forelle" indicates that it was probably composed in early 1817. The several versions differ somewhat, ranging from the 1817 version, which lacks introductory material and has a tempo marking of *Mäßig* [Moderate], to an 1820 version, which has no tempo marking and still no piano introduction. The only authentic copy with a piano introduction is dated October, 1821. Diabelli published the song several times between 1825 and 1829 as Opus 32. Schubert used the melody of "Die Forelle" in the fourth movement of his String Quintet, D 667, (the "Trout") as the theme for a set of variations. See "An den Tod" for notes on Schubart.

Die Forelle

In einem Bächlein helle,
Da schoss in froher Eil
Die launische Forelle
Vorüber wie ein Pfeil.
Ich stand an dem Gestade
Und sah in süßer Ruh
Des muntern Fischleins Bade
Im klaren Bächlein zu.

Ein Fischer mit der Rute
Wohl an dem Ufer stand
Und sah's mit kaltem Blute,
Wie sich das Fischlein wand.
So lang dem Wasser Helle,
So dacht ich, nicht gebricht,
So fängt er die Forelle
Mit seiner Angel nicht.

Doch endlich ward dem Diebe
Die Zeit zu lang. Er macht
Das Bächlein tückisch trübe,
Und eh ich es gedacht,
So zuckte seine Rute,
Das Fischlein zappelt dran,
Und ich mit regem Blute
Sah die Betrogne an.

The Trout

In a clear brook
there darted in joyful haste
the capricious trout
past, like an arrow.
I stood on the bank
and watched, in sweet peace,
the merry little fish's bath
in the clear brook.

A fisherman with his rod
stood right at the edge
and observed, heartlessly,
how the little fish wriggled around.
As long as the clearness of the water—
so thought I—is not lacking,
then he won't catch the trout
with his hook.

But finally became, for the thief,
the waiting time too long. He made
the little brook, maliciously, muddy;
and before I realized it,
he jerked his rod.
The little fish struggled on it;
and I, with quick pulse,
regarded the betrayed one.

ei - nem Bäch - lein hel - le, da schoss in fro-her_ Eil die
Fi - scher mit der Ru - te wohl an dem U - fer_ stand und

lau - ni - sche Fo - rel - le vor - ü - ber_ wie ein Pfeil. Ich
sah's mit kal - tem Blu - te, wie sich das_ Fisch - lein wand. So

stand an dem Ge - sta - de und sah in sü - ßer_ Ruh des
lang dem Was - ser_ Hel - le, so dacht ich, nicht ge - bricht, so

mun - tern Fisch - leins Ba - de im kla - ren Bäch - lein zu, des
fängt er die Fo - rel - le mit sei - ner An - gel nicht, so

trü - be, und eh_____ ich es ge - dacht, so zuck - te sei - ne

Ru - te, das Fisch - lein, das Fisch - lein zap - pelt dran, und

ich mit re - gem Blu - te sah die Be - trog - ne an, und

ich_ mit re - gem_ Blu - te sah die Be - trog - ne an.

Die junge Nonne

poem by Jacob Nicolaus de Jachelutta Craigher

D 828. Original key: F minor. The composition date is believed to be late 1824 or early 1825, based on the evidence of a journal entry by Sophie Müller in March, 1825, indicating that she had sung this "new song" for Schubert. It was published with "Nacht und Träume" as Opus 43, in July, 1825, by A.W. Pennauer. That version had numerous mistakes, and it's possible that in measures 16 and 39 the octave G double-sharp should be changed to G-sharp, making it the same as the vocal line in the measures that follow. Craigher (1797–1855), a self-made man who amassed a fortune, was the poet for three Schubert songs, all written in 1824–25. After acquiring wealth as an Italian merchant, he settled in Vienna in 1820 and became well known to literary circles there. It is believed that Schubert received each of the Craigher poems in manuscript form.

Die junge Nonne	The Young Nun
Wie braust durch die Wipfel der heulende Sturm!	*How rages through the treetops the howling storm!*
Es klirren die Balken, es zittert das Haus!	*The rafters rattle, the house shakes!*
Es rollet der Donner, es leuchtet der Blitz!	*The thunder rolls, the lightning flashes!*
Und finster die Nacht, wie das Grab!	*And dark the night, like the grave!*
Immerhin, immerhin!	*So be it, so be it!*
So tobt' es auch jüngst noch in mir!	*So raved it also, recently, in me!*
Es brauste das Leben, wie jetzo der Sturm!	*Life raged, as now the storm!*
Es bebten die Glieder, wie jetzo das Haus!	*My limbs trembled, as now the house!*
Es flammte die Liebe, wie jetzo der Blitz!	*Love flared, as now the lightning!*
Und finster die Brust, wie das Grab!	*And dark my heart, like the grave!*
Nun tobe, du wilder, gewalt'ger Sturm!	*Now rave, you wild, mighty storm!*
Im Herzen ist Friede, im Herzen ist Ruh!	*In my heart is peace; in my heart is repose!*
Des Bräutigams harret die liebende Braut,	*The loving bride awaits the bridegroom,*
Gereinigt in prüfender Glut—	*purified in the test of fire—*
Der ewigen Liebe getraut.	*to eternal Love betrothed.*
Ich harre, mein Heiland, mit sehnendem Blick;	*I await, my Saviour, with longing eyes;*
Komm, himmlischer Bräutigam! hole die Braut!	*Come, heavenly bridegroom, take the bride!*
Erlöse die Seele von irdischer Haft!	*Release my soul from earthly bonds!*
Horch! friedlich ertönet das Glöcklein vom Turm;	*Hark! Peacefully resounds the bell from the tower;*
Es lockt mich das süße Getön	*the sweet ringing attracts me*
Allmächtig zu ewigen Höhn.	*all-powerfully to eternal heights.*
Alleluja!	*Alleluia!*

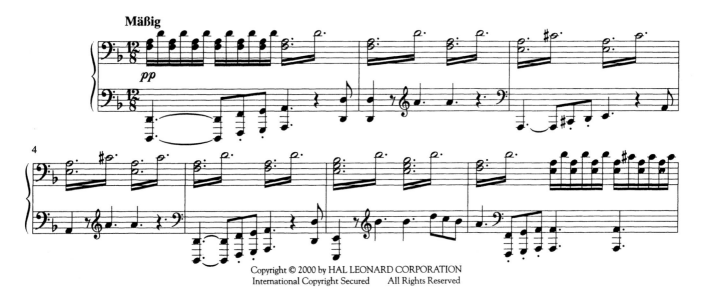

Wie braust durch die Wip - fel der heu - len - de Sturm!

Es klir - ren die Bal - ken, es zit - tert das Haus!

Es rol - let der Don - ner, es leuch - tet der Blitz!

Und fins - ter die Nacht, und

beb - ten die Glie - der, wie jet - zo das Haus! Es flamm - te die Lie - be, wie

jet - zo der Blitz! Und fins - ter die Brust, und

fins - ter die Brust, wie das

Grab! Nun to - be, du wil - der, ge-

Die Männer sind méchant!

poem by Johann Gabriel Seidl

D 866, No. 3. Original key: A minor. This was published by Weigl as the third of the "Vier Refrainlieder" [Four Refrain Songs], Opus 95, in 1828. They were dedicated to the poet by Schubert with the inscription, "in most friendly fashion." Seidl (1804–1875) was a popular writer and well known government official who wrote the modern version of the Austrian national anthem. He enjoyed coin collecting as a hobby. Sometimes referred to as a "patriotic" poet, his collected works, published posthumously, ran to six volumes.

Die Männer sind méchant!	Men Are Cruel

Du sagtest mir es, Mutter:
Er ist ein Springinsfeld!
Ich würd' es dir nicht glauben,
Bis ich mich krank gequält!
Ja, ja, nun ist er's wirklich;
Ich hatt' ihn nur verkannt!
Du sagtest mir's, o Mutter:
»Die Männer sind méchant!«

You told me so, mother:
He is a rogue!
I would not believe you
until I worried myself sick!
Yes, yes, now he really is one;
I had simply misjudged him!
You told me so, oh mother:
"Men are cruel!"

Vorm Dorf, im Busch, als gestern
Die stille Dämm'rung sank,
Da rauscht' es: »Guten Abend!«
Da rauscht' es: »Schönen Dank!«
Ich schlich hinzu, ich horchte;
Ich stand wie festgebannt:
Er war's mit einer andern:
»Die Männer sind méchant!«

Outside the village, in the thicket, as yesterday
the silent dusk descended,
there murmured: "Good evening!"
There murmured: "Many thanks!"
I crept up, I listened;
I stood as if spell-bound:
It was he, with another:
"Men are cruel!"

O Mutter, welche Qualen!
Es muss heraus, es muss!
Es blieb nicht bloß beim Rauschen,
Es blieb nicht bloß beim Gruß.
Vom Gruße kam's zum Kusse;
Vom Kuss zum Druck der Hand;
Vom Druck, ach, liebe Mutter!
»Die Männer sind méchant!«

Oh mother, what torture!
I must come out with it, I must!
It didn't stop merely with murmuring;
it didn't stop merely with greeting.
From greeeting it went to kisses,
from kiss to a squeeze of the hand;
from the squeeze…alas, dear mother!
"Men are cruel!"

Du sag - test mir es,
Vorm Dorf, im Busch, als
O Mut - ter, wel - che

Mut - ter: Er ist ein Spring - ins - feld!   Ich
ges - tern die stil - le Dämm'-rung sank,   da
Qua - len! Es muss her - aus, es muss!   Es

würd' es dir nicht glau - ben, bis ich mich krank ge -
rauscht' es: »Gu - ten A - bend!« Da rauscht' mich: »Schö - nen
blieb nicht bloß beim Rau - schen, es blieb nicht bloß beim

quält!   Ja, ja, nun ist er's wirk - lich; ich
Dank!«   Ich schlich hin - zu, ich horch - te; ich
Gruß.   Vom Gru - ße kam's zum Kus - se; vom

Die liebe Farbe

poem by Wilhelm Müller

D 795, No. 16. Original key: B minor. This is the sixteenth song of the cycle *Die schöne Müllerin*. See "Der Neugierige" for notes on Müller and *Die schöne Müllerin*.

Die liebe Farbe	The Beloved Color
In Grün will ich mich kleiden,	In green will I dress myself,
In grüne Tränenweiden,	in green weeping willows;
Mein Schatz hat's Grün so gern.	my sweetheart is so fond of green.
Will suchen einen Zypressenhain,	I will search for a cypress grove,
Eine Heide von grünem Rosmarein,	a heath of green rosemary;
Mein Schatz hat's Grün so gern.	my sweetheart is so fond of green.
Wohlauf zum fröhlichen Jagen,	Off now to the merry hunt!
Wohlauf durch Heid' und Hagen,	Off through heath and grove!
Mein Schatz hat's Jagen so gern.	My sweetheart is so fond of hunting.
Das Wild, das ich jage, das ist der Tod,	The game that I hunt—it is death;
Die Heide, die heiß ich die Liebesnot,	the heath—I call it "love's affliction."
Mein Schatz hat's Jagen so gern.	My sweetheart is so fond of hunting.
Grabt mir ein Grab im Wasen,	Dig for me a grave in the turf;
Deckt mich mit grünem Rasen,	cover me with green grass.
Mein Schatz hat's Grün so gern.	My sweetheart is so fond of green.
Kein Kreuzlein schwarz, kein Blümlein bunt,	No little black cross, no colorful little flower;
Grün, alles grün so rings umher,	green, everything green, all around!
Mein Schatz hat's Grün so gern.	My sweetheart is so fond of green.

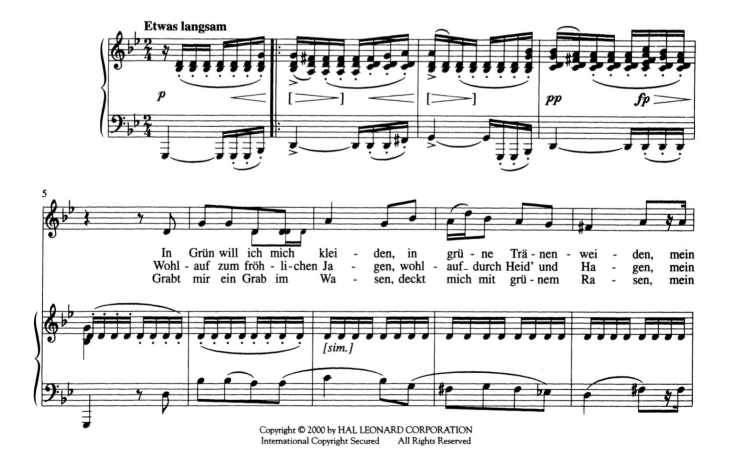

Die Liebe hat gelogen

poem by Karl August Graf von Platen-Hallermünde

D 751. Original key: C minor. Schubert became acquainted with Platen's poetry through Franz Bruchmann, who met Platen in early 1821. This song was composed in the spring of 1822. There are no autographs, and the chronology of its creation can only be deduced from a series of letters which passed between the poet and Bruchmann from September, 1821, to April, 1822. The original poem consisted of just two verses, as reproduced below, but Schubert chose to repeat the first verse as a kind of musical bookend. The song was published as Opus 23, No. 1, by Sauer and Leidesdorf, in August of 1823. Platen (1796–1835) was both poet and playwright. He was born into a wealthy family who had planned a military career for him, but once commissioned he found military life not to his liking and was decommissioned in 1818. From then on his focus was poetry and world travel. Also see "Du liebst mich nicht." See "Am See" for notes on Bruchmann.

Die Liebe hat gelogen	Love Has Lied
Die Liebe hat gelogen,	Love has lied;
Die Sorge lastet schwer,	sorrow weighs heavily.
Betrogen, ach, betrogen	Deceived—alas, deceived
Hat alles mich umher.	by everyone around me.
Es fließen heiße Tropfen	Hot tears flow
Die Wange stets herab,	ever down my cheeks.
Lass ab, mein Herz, zu klopfen,	Cease, my heart, to beat;
Du armes Herz, lass ab.	you poor heart, cease.

Die Unterscheidung

poem by Johann Gabriel Seidl

D 866, No. 1. Original key: G major. This was published as the first of the "Vier Refrainlieder." When first published in the Almanac *Das Veilchen*, in 1835, the poem was titled, "Gretchens Abscheu vor der Liebe" [Gretchen's Abhorrence of Love]. See "Die Männer sind méchant!" for notes on Seidl and the "Vier Refrainlieder."

Die Unterscheidung

Die Mutter hat mich jüngst gescholten
Und vor der Liebe streng gewarnt.
»Noch jede,« sprach sie, »hat's entgolten:
Verloren ist, wen sie umgarnt!«
Drum ist es besser, wie ich meine,
Wenn keins von uns davon mehr spricht;
Ich bin zwar immer noch die Deine,
Doch lieben, Hans! lieben kann ich dich nicht!

Vor Allem, Hans, vergiss mir nimmer,
Dass du nur mich zu lieben hast.
Mein Lächeln sei dir Lust nur immer
Und jeder andern Lächeln Last!
Ja, um der Mutter nachzugeben,
Will ich mich, treu der Doppelpflicht,
Dir zu gefallen stets bestreben,
Doch lieben, Hans! lieben kann ich dich nicht!

Bei jedem Feste, das wir haben,
Soll's meine größte Wonne sein,
Flicht deine Hand des Frühlings Gaben
Zum Schmucke mir ins Mieder ein.
Beginnt der Tanz, dann ist, wie billig,
Ein Tanz mit Gretchen deine Pflicht;
Selbst eifersüchtig werden will ich,
Doch lieben, Hans! lieben kann ich dich nicht!

Und sinkt der Abend kühl hernieder,
Und ruhn wir dann, recht mild bewegt,
Halt immer mir die Hand ans Mieder,
Und fühle, wie mein Herzchen schlägt!
Und willst du mich durch Küsse lehren,
Was stumm dein Auge zu mir spricht,
Selbst das will ich dir nicht verwehren,
Doch lieben, Hans! lieben kann ich dich nicht!

The Distinction

Mother has recently scolded me
and sternly warned me against love.
"Every woman," said she, "has suffered for it:
Lost is she whom it ensnares!"
Therefore it is better, so I think,
if neither of us speaks of it anymore.
I am, to be sure, always still yours;
but to love, Hans? Love you I can not!

Above all, Hans, forget me never—
that you have only me to love.
May my smile be your only pleasure, always,
and those others' smiles oppressive!
Yes, in order to give in to mother
will I, true to my double-duty,
always endeavor to please you.
But to love, Hans? Love you I can not!

At every holiday that we have
it should be my greatest joy if
your hand entwines the gifts of spring
as adornment upon my bodice.
When the dance begins—then is, as is fair,
a dance with Gretchen your duty;
I will even become jealous.
But to love, Hans? Love you I can not!

And when the cool evening descends,
and we rest then, very tenderly moved with emotion,
hold, ever, your hand upon my bodice,
and feel how my heart beats!
And if you want, through kisses, to teach me
what, silently, your eyes speak to me,
even that will I not forbid you.
But to love, Hans? Love you I can not.

Die Mut - ter hat mich jüngst ge-schol-ten und
Vor Al - lem, Hans, ver - giss mir nim-mer, dass

p

vor der Lie - be streng- ge-warnt.
du nur mich zu lie - ben hast.

»Noch je - de,« sprach sie,
Mein Lä - cheln sei dir

»hat's ent - gol - ten: Ver - lo - ren ist,___ wen sie___ um-garnt, ver -
Lust nur im - mer und je - der an - dern Lä - cheln Last, und

lo - ren ist,___ wen sie___ um - garnt!«___
je - der an - dern Lä - cheln Last!___

rit.   *a tempo*

Drum ist es bes - ser,
Ja, um der Mut - ter

rit.   *pp a tempo*

Du bist die Ruh

poem by Friedrich Rückert

D 776. Original key: E-flat major. In 1822 Rückert published a collection of untitled poems called *Östliche Rosen* [Oriental Roses]. From this collection Schubert chose three to set to music, giving them titles of his own devising. "Du bist die Ruh," written possibly as early as 1822, wasn't published until September, 1826, by Sauer and Leidesdorf, in a collection called "Four Songs by Rückert and Graf Platten." For a later edition of the poems Rückert gave this poem the title, "Kehr' ein bei mir" [Commune with Me]. See "Dass sie hier gewesen!" for notes on Rückert. Also see "Lachen und Weinen."

Du bist die Ruh	*You Are Rest*
Du bist die Ruh,	*You are rest,*
Der Friede mild,	*gentle peace;*
Die Sehnsucht du,	*the longing, you,*
Und was sie stillt.	*and that which satisfies it.*
Ich weihe dir	*I consecrate to you,*
Voll Lust und Schmerz	*full of joy and sorrow,*
Zur Wohnung hier	*as a dwelling place here,*
Mein Aug und Herz.	*my eyes and heart.*
Kehr ein bei mir,	*Come commune with me,*
Und schließe du	*and close*
Still hinter dir	*quietly behind you*
Die Pforten zu.	*the gates.*
Treib andern Schmerz	*Drive other pain*
Aus dieser Brust.	*from this breast.*
Voll sei dies Herz	*Full may this heart be*
Von deiner Lust.	*of your joy.*
Dies Augenzelt,	*The temple of these eyes*
Von deinem Glanz	*from your radiance*
Allein erhellt,	*alone brightens;*
O füll es ganz.	*oh, fill it completely.*

o füll es ganz, o füll es ganz.

Dies Au - gen - zelt, von dei - nem Glanz al -

lein er - hellt, o füll es ganz,

o füll es ganz.

Du liebst mich nicht

poem by Karl August Graf von Platen-Hallermünde

D 756. Original key: A minor. This song was composed in 1822 and published in September of 1826, by Sauer and Leidesdorf, as Opus 59, No. 1. It was transposed to A minor from the autograph's G-sharp minor, the only known use of that key by Schubert in his songs. Opus 59 also included "Die Liebe hat gelogen" and three Rückert settings. The Platen poems (Schubert set only two) came from a volume entitled, *Ghaselen.* A "ghazal" (See "Sei mir gegrüßt") is an oriental verse form, indicating that Platen, like Rückert, had an interest in the languages and poetry of the orient. See "Die Liebe hat gelogen" for notes on Platen.

Du liebst mich nicht

Mein Herz ist zerrissen, du liebst mich nicht,
Du ließest mich's wissen, du liebst mich nicht!
Wiewohl ich dir flehend und werbend erschien,
Und liebebeflissen, du liebst mich nicht!
Du hast es gesprochen, mit Worten gesagt,
Mit allzu gewissen, du liebst mich nicht.
So soll ich die Sterne, so soll ich den Mond,
Die Sonne vermissen? Du liebst mich nicht!
Was blüht mir die Rose? was blüht der Jasmin?
Was blühn die Narzissen? Du liebst mich nicht.

You Love Me Not

My heart is broken; you love me not.
You have let me know it—you love me not!
Although I appeared before you, pleading and wooing,
and zealous with love, you love me not!
You have said it, with words spoken,
with words all too clear: you love me not.
So must I the stars, so must I the moon,
the sun forego? You love me not!
Why blooms for me the rose? Why blooms the jasmine?
Why blooms the narcissus? You love me not.

Ster - ne, so soll ich den Mond, die Son - ne ver - mis - sen? Du liebst, du liebst mich

nicht! Was blüht mir die Ro - se? was blüht der Jas - min? was blühn die Nar -

zis - sen? Du liebst, du liebst mich nicht, du liebst, du liebst mich

nicht.

Ellens Gesang I (Raste Krieger)

poem by Sir Walter Scott/Adam Storck

D 837. Original key: D-flat major. The three "Ellen" songs are among five Schubert set for solo voice using texts from Scott's *The Lady of the Lake*. Scott's narrative, written in 1810, was successful throughout Europe and was translated into German by Adam Storck, a Bremen professor, in 1819. It was Schubert's intention to publish the songs with both the German and original English texts to capitalize on Scott's fame and perhaps make himself better known outside of Austria. This was done, with the English printed just below the German, but his reputation was not enhanced. All three songs were written in 1825. Though the precise dates of their origin are uncertain, Schubert began work on them in April, and they were performed three months later in Gmunden, by Schubert and his singing colleague, Vogl. They were published as Opus 52, by Artaria in April, 1826. The first, a lullaby to a soldier at rest, was prefaced with: "She sung, and still a harp unseen/Filled up the symphony between." The songs were dedicated to Schubert's friend and admirer, Sofie, Countess Weißenwolf of Steyregg. Scott (1771–1832), a Scottish poet and the quintessential Romantic novelist in the English language, was the creator of the historical novel. After successfully writing a number of popular narrative poems he went on to complete 28 novels, including his most enduring, *Ivanhoe*. See "Ganymed" for notes on Vogl.

Ellens Gesang I Raste Krieger	*Ellen's Song I* *Rest, Warrior*
Raste Krieger, Krieg ist aus, Schlaf den Schlaf, nichts wird dich wecken, Träume nicht von wildem Strauß, Nicht von Tag und Nacht voll Schrecken,	*Rest, warrior! Your war is over.* *Sleep the sleep; nothing will wake you.* *Dream not of fierce combat,* *not of day and night full of horror.*
In der Insel Zauberhallen Wird ein weicher Schlafgesang Um das müde Haupt dir wallen Zu der Zauberharfe Klang.	*In the island's magic halls* *will a soft lullaby* *around your weary head undulate* *to the sound of the magic harp.*
Feen mit unsichtbaren Händen Werden auf dein Lager hin Holde Schlummerblumen senden, Die im Zauberlande blühn.	*Fairies with invisible hands* *will to your couch there* *send lovely flowers of slumber* *which bloom in the magic land.*
Nicht der Trommel wildes Rasen, Nicht des Kriegs gebietend Wort, Nicht der Todeshörner Blasen Scheuchen deinen Schlummer fort.	*Not the wild fury of drums,* *not the summoning call to war,* *not the sounding of bugles of death* *shall frighten your slumber away.*
Nicht das Stampfen wilder Pferde, Nicht der Schreckensruf der Wacht, Nicht das Bild von Tagsbeschwerde Stören deine stille Nacht.	*Not the stomping of fierce horses,* *not the frightened cry of the guard,* *not the vision of daily hardships* *shall disturb your quiet night.*
Doch der Lerche Morgensänge Wecken sanft dein schlummernd Ohr, Und des Sumpfgefieders Klänge, Steigend aus Geschilf und Rohr.	*But the lark's morning songs* *will gently wake your slumbering ear,* *and the sound of the marsh birds,* *rising from reeds and rushes.*

Ras - te Krie - ger, Krieg ist aus, schlaf____ den

Schlaf,____ nichts wird____ dich we - cken, träu - me nicht von wil - dem

Strauß,____ nicht von Tag____ und____ Nacht____ voll Schre - cken, schlaf den

Schlaf, nichts wird dich we - cken, träu - me nicht von wil - dem Strauß,____ nicht von

Tag— und— Nacht— voll Schre - cken.

Langsam

In der In - sel Zau - ber -

dim.   *pp*

hal - len wird ein wei - cher Schlaf - ge - sang um das mü - de— Haupt dir—

wal - len zu der Zau - ber - har - fe— Klang,— wird ein wei - cher— Schlaf - ge - sang dir

ppp

Strauß,— nicht von Tag— und— Nacht— voll— Schre - cken, schlaf den

Schlaf, nichts wird dich we - cken, träu - me nicht von wil - dem Strauß,— nicht von

Tag— und— Nacht— voll— Schre - cken.

Geschwind

Nicht der Trom - mel wil - des

dim. *p*

138
sanft dein— schlum-mernd Ohr.

142 **Mäßig**
Ras - te Krie - ger, Krieg ist—

147
aus, schlaf——— den Schlaf,— nichts wird——— dich— we - cken, träu-me

152
nicht von wil-dem Strauß,— nicht von Tag——— und— Nacht—— voll— Schre -

Ellens Gesang II (Jäger, ruhe von der Jagd!)

poem by Sir Walter Scott/Adam Storck

D 838. Original key: E-flat major. The text of this song follows the text of "Ellens Gesang I" in Scott's poem, *The Lady of the Lake*. See "Ellens Gesang I" for notes on Scott and Storck. Also see "Ellens Gesang III."

Ellens Gesang II Jäger, ruhe von der Jagd!	Ellen's Song II *Hunter, Rest from the Hunt!*
Jäger, ruhe von der Jagd! Weicher Schlummer soll dich decken, Träume nicht, wenn Sonn' erwacht, Dass Jagdhörner dich erwecken.	*Hunter, rest from the hunt!* *Gentle slumber shall cover you;* *Dream not that when the sun awakes,* *hunting horns will awake you.*
Schlaf, der Hirsch ruht in der Höhle, Bei dir sind die Hunde wach, Schlaf, nicht quäl es deine Seele, Dass dein edles Roß erlag.	*Sleep! The stag rests in his den;* *beside you your hounds are wide-awake.* *Sleep; let it not torture your soul* *that your noble horse has died.*
Jäger, ruhe von der Jagd! Weicher Schlummer soll dich decken, Wenn der junge Tag erwacht, Wird kein Jägerhorn dich wecken.	*Hunter, rest from the hunt!* *Gentle slumber shall cover you;* *when the new day dawns* *will no hunting horn wake you.*

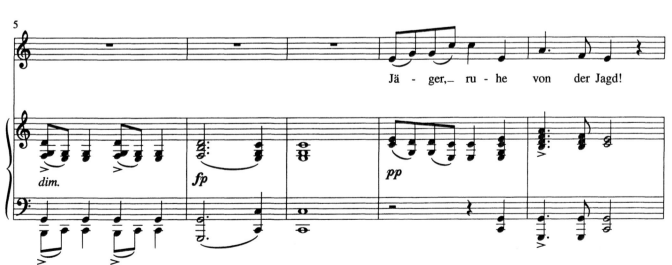

Ellens Gesang III (Ave Maria!)

poem by Sir Walter Scott/Adam Storck

D 839. Original key: B-flat major. This celebrated song, known also as "Hymne an die Jungfrau," is presumably Ellen singing to her own harp accompaniment as she prays to the Virgin Mary. In a letter to his parents, dated July 25, 1825, Schubert spoke of the song's early success: "We played, among others, some of my new songs from Walter Scott's *Lady of the Lake*. The hymn to the blessed Virgin was particularly well received…it seems to touch all hearts, and inspires a feeling of devotion. I believe the reason is that I never force myself to be devout, and never compose hymns or prayers of that sort except when the mood takes me; but then it is usually the right and true devotion." See "Ellens Gesang I" for notes on Scott and Storck. Also see "Ellens Gesang II."

Ellens Gesang III
Hymne an die Jungfrau

Ave Maria! Jungfrau mild,
Erhöre einer Jungfrau Flehen,
Aus diesem Felsen, starr und wild,
Soll mein Gebet zu dir hinwehen.
Wir schlafen sicher bis zum Morgen,
Ob Menschen noch so grausam sind.
O Jungfrau, sieh der Jungfrau Sorgen,
O Mutter, hör ein bittend Kind!
Ave Maria!

Ave Maria! Unbefleckt!
Wenn wir auf diesen Fels hinsinken
Zum Schlaf, und uns dein Schutz bedeckt,
Wird weich der harte Fels uns dünken.
Du lächelst, Rosendüfte wehen
In dieser dumpfen Felsenkluft.
O Mutter, höre Kindes Flehen,
O Jungfrau, eine Jungfrau ruft!
Ave Maria!

Ave Maria! Reine Magd!
Der Erde und der Luft Dämonen,
Von deines Auges Huld verjagt,
Sie können hier nicht bei uns wohnen!
Wir woll'n uns still dem Schicksal beugen,
Da uns dein heil'ger Trost anweht,
Der Jungfrau wolle hold dich neigen,
Dem Kind, das für den Vater fleht!
Ave Maria!

Ellen's Song III
Hymn to the Virgin

Hail Mary! Virgin mild,
grant the entreaties of a maiden;
from this rock, rigid and wild,
shall my prayer waft to you.
We shall sleep safely until morning,
however men are yet so dreaded.
Oh Virgin, see the maiden's sorrows;
oh mother, hear a supplicating child!
Hail Mary!

Hail Mary! Undefiled!
When we sink down upon this rock
in sleep, and your protection shelters us,
the hard rock seems soft to us.
You smile; the scent of roses wafts
through this murky chasm.
Oh mother, hear a child's entreaties;
oh Virgin, a maiden cries out!
Hail Mary!

Hail Mary! Chaste maid!
Demons of the earth and of the air,
by the grace of your eyes expelled—
they can not dwell with us here!
We wish to submit quietly to fate,
as your holy comfort comes over us.
To a maiden be willing, graciously, to incline yourself,
to the child who prays for its father!
Hail Mary!

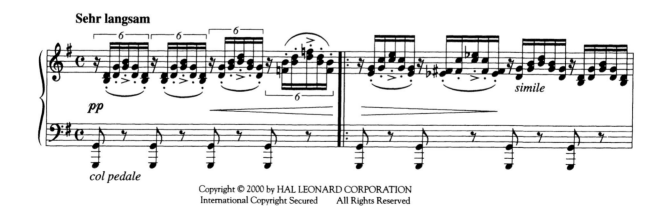

Men - schen noch so grau - sam sind. O Jung - frau, sieh der Jung - frau
die - ser dump - fen Fel - sen - kluft. O Mut - ter, hö - re Kin - des
uns dein heil' - ger Trost an - weht, der Jung - frau wol - le hold dich

Sor - gen, o Mut - ter, hör ein bit - tend Kind!
Fle - hen, o Jung - frau, ei - ne Jung - frau ruft!
nei - gen, dem Kind, das für den Va - ter fleht!

A - ve Ma - ri - a!
A - ve Ma - ri - a!
A - ve Ma - ri - a!

Erlafsee

poem by Johann Baptist Mayrhofer

D 586. Original key: F major. Written in September of 1817, and first published on February 6, 1818, in *Mahlerisches Tashenbuch* [Pictorial Pocket Book] under the title "Am Erlafsee," this was Schubert's first published composition. The song was later reissued by Cappi and Diabelli in May, 1822, as Opus 8, No. 3, with its present title, and dedicated "with great respect" to Johann Karl, Count Esterhazy. The original poem was thirty-six lines long, but Schubert set only fourteen lines, repeating the first two at the end. See "Abendstern" for notes on Mayrhofer.

Erlafsee	*Lake Erlaf*
Mir ist so wohl, so weh	*I feel so happy, so sad*
Am stillen Erlafsee.	*by the quiet Lake Erlaf.*
Heilig Schweigen	*Hallowed silence*
In Fichtenzweigen,	*midst firs' branches;*
Regungslos	*motionless*
Der blaue Schoß,	*the blue lap;*
Nur der Wolken Schatten fliehn	*only the clouds' shadows flee along*
Überm dunklen Spiegel hin.	*over the dark mirror.*
Frische Winde	*Cool breezes*
Kräuseln linde	*ruffle gently*
Das Gewässer;	*the water;*
Und der Sonne	*and the sun's*
Güldne Krone	*golden crown*
Flimmert blässer.	*glimmers paler.*

güld - ne Kro - ne, und____ der Son - ne güld - ne

Kro - ne flim - mert bläs - ser. Mir_ ist so wohl,_ so

weh am_ stil - len Er - laf - see, mir_ ist so wohl,_ so

weh am_ stil - len Er - laf - see.

Erster Verlust

poem by Johann Wolfgang von Goethe

D 226. Original key: F minor. This song was written in 1815. A copy made for Goethe in 1816 is in 2/2. The song was published in July, 1821, by Cappi and Diabelli along with four other Goethe settings ("Rastlose Liebe," "Nähe des Geliebten," "Der Fischer," and "Der König in Thule") as Opus 5. This published version differs slightly from the only known autograph, now in a monastery in Austria, but it's assumed the alterations are Schubert's own. Schubert dedicated the song to his teacher, Anton Salieri. See "An den Mond" for notes on Goethe.

Erster Verlust	First Loss
Ach, wer bringt die schönen Tage,	*Ah, who will bring the beautiful days,*
Jene Tage der ersten Liebe,	*those days of first love…*
Ach, wer bringt nur eine Stunde	*ah, who will bring but one hour*
Jener holden Zeit zurück!	*of that lovely time back!*
Einsam nähr' ich meine Wunde,	*Alone I nurture my wound,*
Und mit stets erneuter Klage	*and with ever renewed lament*
Traur' ich ums verlorne Glück.	*I grieve for the lost happiness.*
Ach, wer bringt die schönen Tage,	*Ah, who will bring the beautiful days,*
Wer jene holde Zeit zurück!	*who [will bring] that lovely time back!*

je - ner hol - den Zeit— zu - rück! Ein - sam nähr'— ich mei - ne

Wun - de, und mit stets er - neu - ter— Kla - ge traur'

ich ums ver - lor - ne Glück. Ach, wer bringt die schö - nen—

Ta - ge, wer je - ne hol - de Zeit— zu - rück!

Frühlingsglaube

poem by Johann Ludwig Uhland

D 686. Original key: A-flat major. This song, (Schubert's only Uhland setting) in its earliest version, dated September, 1820, is in the key of B-flat major and has no real piano introduction. The first "revision" is still in B-flat and has the tempo marking, *Mäßig* [Moderate]. The third version, dated 1820, keeps the key and tempo marking, but adds the present piano introduction. The final copy, made for Sauer and Leidesdorf, is transposed to A-flat major and is dated November, 1822. It was published in April, 1823, as Opus 20, No. 2, and is dedicated to Justine von Bruchmann, sister of Schubert's friend, Franz von Bruchmann. Uhland (1787–1862), poet and playwright, studied law but practiced only a short time. After developing an interest in mythology, medieval literature and folklore, he accepted an appointment as Professor of German Literature at Tübingen. His own ballads and songs were an important influence on the younger poets of his time and are still well known. See "Am See" for notes on Bruchmann.

Frühlingsglaube	*Faith in Spring*
Die linden Lüfte sind erwacht,	*The balmy breezes are awakened.*
Sie säuseln und weben Tag und Nacht,	*They whisper and flutter day and night;*
Sie schaffen an allen Enden.	*they are creative all around.*
O frischer Duft, o neuer Klang,	*Oh fresh fragrance, oh new sound!*
Nun armes Herze, sei nicht bang,	*Now, poor heart, be not fearful!*
Nun muss sich alles, alles wenden.	*Now must everything, everything change.*
Die Welt wird schöner mit jedem Tag,	*The world becomes more beautiful with each day.*
Man weiß nicht, was noch werden mag,	*One knows not what still may be to come.*
Das Blühen will nicht enden,	*The flowering will not end;*
Es will nicht enden.	*it will not end.*
Es blüht das fernste, tiefste Tal,	*The most distant, deepest valley blooms.*
Nun armes Herz, vergiss der Qual,	*Now, poor heart, forget the pain.*
Nun muss sich alles, alles wenden.	*Now must everything, everything change.*

Die lin - den Lüf - te sind er - wacht, sie

säu - seln und we - ben Tag_ und_ Nacht, sie schaf - fen an al - len En - den, an_

al - len En - den. O fri - scher Duft, o neu - er Klang,

o neu - er Klang, nun ar - mes Her - ze,

sei nicht bang, nun muss sich al - les, al - les wen - den, nun muss sich al - les,

cresc.

al - les _ wen - den.

Die Welt wird schö - ner mit je - dem_ Tag, man

weiß nicht, was__ noch wer - den_ mag, Das Blü - hen will nicht en - den, es__

will nicht en - den. Es blüht das_ ferns - te, tiefs - te Tal,

Ganymed

poem by Johann Wolfgang von Goethe

D 544. Original key: A-flat major. In the mythological story, Ganymede was carried to heaven by an eagle, as commanded by Zeus. The beautiful youth was to be a cup bearer for the gods. Goethe's poem was written in 1774. "Ganymed" was composed in March, 1817, and published in 1825 by Diabelli, as Opus 19, No. 3. The original tempo marking, *Etwas geschwind* [Somewhat fast], was changed to *Etwas langsam* [Somewhat slow]. While this change was probably Schubert's, the published dedication to Goethe was made without Schubert's permission. It is believed that this song firmed the friendship between Schubert and the talented baritone, Johann Michael Vogl. Vogl (1768–1840) was a popular singer in Vienna and the most important Schubertian singer of his time. Schubert first heard his talents in a performance as Orestes in *Iphigénie en Tauride* in 1813. At their first meeting, in 1817, Schubert showed the baritone three songs, and from that time considered him the ideal interpreter of his work. Schubert once wrote to his brother, Ferdinand, "The way and manner in which Vogl sings and I accompany, so that we seem in such a moment to be one, is something quite new and unheard of to these people." Vogl premiered "Erlkönig" before its 1821 publication, and shortly before his death performed *Winterreise* complete. He died on the twelfth anniversary of Schubert's death. See "An den Mond" for notes on Goethe.

Ganymed	Ganymede
Wie im Morgenglanze	*How, in the morning's splendor,*
Du rings mich anglühst,	*you glow all around me,*
Frühling, Geliebter!	*spring, beloved!*
Mit tausendfacher Liebeswonne	*With love's thousandfold rapture*
Sich an mein Herze drängt	*presses upon my heart*
Deiner ewigen Wärme	*your eternal warmth's*
Heilig Gefühl,	*divine feeling,*
Unendliche Schöne!	*endless beauty!*
Dass ich dich fassen möcht	*Would that I could hold you*
In diesen Arm!	*in these arms!*
Ach, an deinem Busen	*Ah, at your breast*
Lieg ich, und schmachte,	*I lie and languish;*
Und deine Blumen, dein Gras	*and your flowers, your grass*
Drängen sich an mein Herz.	*press against my heart.*
Du kühlst den brennenden	*You cool the burning*
Durst meines Busens,	*thirst of my bosom,*
Lieblicher Morgenwind!	*lovely morning breeze!*
Ruft drein die Nachtigall	*Therein calls the nightingale*
Liebend nach mir aus dem Nebeltal.	*lovingly to me from the misty valley.*
Ich komm! ich komme!	*I come, I come!*
Ach! wohin? wohin?	*Ah, whither? Whither?*
Hinauf strebt's, hinauf!	*Upward I soar, upward!*
Es schweben die Wolken	*The clouds float*
Abwärts, die Wolken	*downward; the clouds*
Neigen sich der sehnenden Liebe.	*bow down to yearning love—*
Mir! Mir!	*to me! To me!*
In eurem Schoße	*Into your lap,*
Aufwärts!	*upwards!*
Umfangend umfangen!	*Embracing, embraced!*
Aufwärts an deinen Busen,	*Upwards to your bosom,*
Allliebender Vater!	*all-loving Father!*

Wär - me hei - lig Ge - fühl, un - end -

- li - che Schö - ne! Dass ich dich fas - sen möcht

in die - sen Arm!___ Ach, an dei - nem Bu - sen lieg ich, und

schmach - te, und dei - ne Blu - men, dein Gras drän -

gen sich an___ mein Herz.

Du kühlst den bren - nen-den Durst mei - nes Bu-sens,

lieb - li - cher Mor - gen - wind!

Ruft drein die

Nach - ti - gall lie - bend nach mir aus dem Ne - bel - tal.

Ich komm! ich kom - me! ach! wo-

hin?___ wo - hin?___ Hin - auf strebt's, hin-

auf! Hin - auf strebt's, hin - auf! Es schwe - ben die Wol - ken

Erlkönig

poem by Johann Wolfgang von Goethe

D 328. Original key: G minor. It's believed Schubert wrote this song at his parents' home in October of 1815. He was only 18. The title comes from "Erlkönigs Tochter" [Erl-king's Daughter], the 1779 translation of a Danish ballad. Johann Gottfried Herder, the translator and a poet in his own right, rendered the Danish *ellerkonge* [king of the elves] as *Erlkönig*. Schubert's text was originally part of a Goethe singspiel, Die Fischerin, and is sung by a fisherwoman as she works. The situation is reminiscent of Goethe's treatment of Gretchen in *Faust*. There are four known copies: The first, the autograph, though missing, is now represented by two copies in good condition. There is also a copy which was made for Goethe in 1816, with a simplified accompaniment featuring eighths instead of triplets. An 1817 copy, sent to Breitkopf and Härtel, was accidentally returned to another man named Franz Schubert, also a composer, living in Dresden, who was angry that the piece could have been confused as his own and claimed no responsibility for it. That copy is now in New York. The fourth, published as Opus 1 by Cappi and Diabelli in March, 1821, is now lost. "Erlkönig" is probably the song most responsible for Schubert's fame during his lifetime. It made an immediate impression on his circle of friends and was performed regularly at the weekly evening musical parlor events which became known as "Schubertiades." See "An den Mond" for notes on Goethe.

Erlkönig	Erl-king
Wer reitet so spät durch Nacht und Wind?	*Who rides so late through night and wind?*
Es ist der Vater mit seinem Kind;	*It is the father with his child.*
Er hat den Knaben wohl in dem Arm,	*He has the boy in his arms;*
Er fasst ihn sicher, er hält ihn warm.	*he holds him securely, he keeps him warm.*
Mein Sohn, was birgst du so bang dein Gesicht?—	*"My son, why do you hide your face so fearfully?"*
Siehst, Vater, du den Erlkönig nicht?	*"Father, don't you see the Erl-king,*
Den Erlenkönig mit Kron' und Schweif?—	*the Erl-king with crown and train?"*
Mein Sohn, es ist ein Nebelstreif.—	*"My son, it is a streak of mist."*
»Du liebes Kind, komm, geh mit mir!	*"You dear child, come, go with me!*
Gar schöne Spiele spiel ich mit dir;	*Very fine games I will play with you;*
Manch bunte Blumen sind an dem Strand;	*many colorful flowers are along the shore;*
Meine Mutter hat manch gülden Gewand.«	*my mother has many golden garments."*
Mein Vater, mein Vater, und hörest du nicht,	*"My father, my father, don't you hear*
Was Erlenkönig mir leise verspricht?—	*what the Erl-king softly promises me?"*
Sei ruhig, bleibe ruhig, mein Kind;	*"Be calm, stay calm, my child;*
In dürren Blättern säuselt der Wind.—	*in the dry leaves whispers the wind."*
»Willst, feiner Knabe, du mit mir gehn?	*"Will you, fine lad, go with me?*
Meine Töchter sollen dich warten schön;	*My daughters will wait on you nicely;*
Meine Töchter führen den nächtlichen Reihn,	*my daughters lead the nightly dance*
Und wiegen und tanzen und singen dich ein.«	*and will rock you and dance you and sing you to sleep."*
Mein Vater, mein Vater, und siehst du nicht dort	*"My father, my father, can't you see there*
Erlkönigs Töchter am düstern Ort?—	*the Erl-king's daughters in that gloomy spot?"*
Mein Sohn, mein Sohn, ich seh es genau;	*"My son, my son, I see it clearly;*
Es scheinen die alten Weiden so grau.—	*the ancient willows glimmer so grey."*
»Ich liebe dich, mich reizt deine schöne Gestalt,	*"I love you; your fair form charms me;*
Und bist du nicht willig, so brauch ich Gewalt.«	*and if you are not willing, then I will use force."*
Mein Vater, mein Vater, jetzt fasst er mich an!	*"My father, my father, now he is seizing me!*
Erlkönig hat mir ein Leids getan!—	*The Erl-king has hurt me!"*
Dem Vater grauset's, er reitet geschwind,	*The father is horrified; he rides swiftly;*
Er hält in Armen das ächzende Kind,	*he holds in his arms the moaning child.*
Erreicht den Hof mit Müh' und Not;	*He reaches the courtyard with effort and strain;*
In seinen Armen das Kind war tot.	*in his arms the child was dead.*

Schnell

Wer rei - tet so spät durch Nacht und

Wind? Es ist der Va - ter mit sei - nem

221

spiel___ ich mit dir; manch bun - te Blu - men sind___ an dem Strand; mei - ne Mut - ter hat___ manch gül - den Ge - wand.« Mein Va - ter, mein Va - ter, und hö - rest du nicht, was Er - len - kö - nig mir lei - se ver-

94

sin - gen dich ein, sie wie - gen und tan - zen und sin - gen dich ein.«

97

Mein Va - ter, mein Va - ter, und siehst du nicht dort Erl -

102

kö - nigs Töch - ter am düs - tern Ort?— Mein Sohn, mein

decresc.

107

Sohn, ich seh es ge - nau; es schei - nen die al - ten Wei - den so

cresc.

Geheimes

poem by Johann Wolfgang von Goethe

D 719. Original key: A-flat major. The poem's original title, "Glückliches Geheimes," was changed by Schubert in the autograph, dated March, 1821. The song was published in December, 1822, by Cappi and Diabelli as Opus 14, No. 2, and was dedicated by the composer to his friend and collaborator, Franz von Schober. See "An die Musik" for notes on Schober. See "An den Mond" for notes on Goethe.

Geheimes

Über meines Liebchens Äugeln
Stehn verwundert alle Leute,
Ich, der Wissende, dagegen
Weiß recht gut, was das bedeute.

Denn es heißt: Ich liebe diesen,
Und nicht etwa den und jenen,
Lasset nur, ihr guten Leute,
Euer Wundern, euer Sehnen.

Ja, mit ungeheuren Mächten
Blicket sie wohl in die Runde;
Doch sie sucht nur zu verkünden
Ihm die nächste süße Stunde.

Secret

Concerning my sweetheart's ogling,
all people are astonished;
I, the knowing one, on the contrary
know very well what that means.

For it means: I love this one,
and not perhaps that one or that other one.
Quit now, you good people,
your marvelling, your longing.

Yes, with mighty powers
she does glance round about;
but she seeks only to make known
to him the next sweet hour.

in die Run - de; doch___ sie sucht nur zu ver - kün - den ihm die nächs - te sü - ße Stun - de, ihm die nächs - te sü - ße___ Stun - - de.

dim.

ppp

f [>] p

pp fp fp pp

Grenzen der Menschheit

poem by Johann Wolfgang von Goethe

D 716. Original key. This song was composed in March, 1821, and published in January, 1832, in Book 14 of *Nachlass* (See "Abendstern"). Though originally written for bass voice, the published version had the voice line in the treble staff. See "An den Mond" for notes on Goethe.

Grenzen der Menschheit	Limitations of Mankind
Wenn der uralte,	When the age-old
Heilige Vater	holy Father,
Mit gelassener Hand	with calm hand
Aus rollenden Wolken	from rolling clouds
Segnende Blitze	beatific lightning flashes
Über die Erde sät,	scatters over the earth,
Küss ich den letzten	I kiss the outermost
Saum seines Kleides,	hem of his robe,
Kindliche Schauer	childlike awe
Tief in der Brust.	deep in my breast.
Denn mit Göttern	For with gods
Soll sich nicht messen	ought a mortal not
Irgend ein Mensch.	ever measure himself.
Hebt er sich aufwärts	If he elevates himself
Und berührt	and touches
Mit dem Scheitel die Sterne,	the stars with the crown of his head,
Nirgends haften dann	nowhere will adhere, in that case,
Die unsichern Sohlen,	the unsteady soles of his feet;
Und mit ihm spielen	and, with him, will toy
Wolken und Winde.	clouds and winds.
Steht er mit festen,	If he stands with firm,
Markigen Knochen	vigorous limbs
Auf der wohlgegründeten,	on the well-grounded,
Dauernden Erde,	enduring earth,
Reicht er nicht auf,	he will not reach up,
Nur mit der Eiche	even with the oak tree
Oder der Rebe	or the vine
Sich zu vergleichen.	to compare himself.
Was unterscheidet	What differentiates
Götter von Menschen?	Gods from men?
Dass viele Wellen	That many waves
Vor jenen wandeln,	roll onward before the former—
Ein ewiger Strom:	an eternal river;
Uns hebt die Welle,	for us the wave rises,
Verschlingt die Welle,	the wave swallows,
Und wir versinken.	and we sink.
Ein kleiner Ring	A small circle
Begrenzt unser Leben,	limits our life;
Und viele Geschlechter	and many generations
Reihen sich dauernd	succeed each other continually
An ihres Daseins	along their existence's
Unendliche Kette.	unending chain.

Nicht ganz langsam

Wenn der ur-al-te, hei-li-ge Va-ter mit ge-las-se-ner

Hand_____ aus rol-len-den_ Wol-ken seg-nen-de

Blit-ze ü-ber die Er-de_ sät, küss ich den letz-ten_

Saum sei - nes Klei - des, kind - li - che Schau - er tief in der Brust,

küss ich den letz - ten Saum sei - nes Klei - des, kind - li - che

Schau - er tief in der Brust.

Denn mit Göt - tern soll sich nicht mes - sen ir - gend ein Mensch.

Hebt er sich auf - wärts und be - rührt mit dem Schei - tel die Ster - ne, nir - gends haf - ten

dann die un - si - chern Soh - len, und mit ihm spie - len Wol - ken und

Win - de; nir - gends haf - ten dann die un - si - chern Soh - len, und

mit ihm spie - len Wol - ken und Win - de.

Gretchen am Spinnrade

poem by Johann Wolfgang von Goethe

D 118. Original key: D minor. The original text comes from Part I of Goethe's *Faust*, as its own scene, "Gretchens Stube" [Gretchen's Room]. The song was written on October 19, 1814, and published by Cappi and Diabelli as Opus 2, in April of 1821. It was dedicated to Count Moritz von Fries, to whom Beethoven also dedicated some early works. "Gretchen am Spinnrade" was the first of seventy-four songs Schubert set to the poetry of Goethe. Schubert repeatedly tried to win the approval of the great Romantic poet and novelist. In 1816, Schubert sent him copies of about twenty selected songs for a proposed volume of Goethe settings. The songs, sent with an introductory letter by Josef von Spaun, were returned without acknowledgment. Schubert tried again in 1825, sending Goethe three songs that are now known as Opus 19, and asking permission to dedicate them to him. There is a diary entry noting Goethe's receipt of the songs but, again, no reply to the composer. Schubert altered the first line of the last verse of the poem on its receipt to, "O könnt' ich ihn küssen" [Oh, if I could kiss him]. See "An den Mond" for notes on Goethe.

Gretchen am Spinnrade	Gretchen at the Spinning Wheel
Meine Ruh ist hin,	My peace is gone,
Mein Herz ist schwer,	my heart is heavy;
Ich finde sie nimmer	I will find it never
Und nimmermehr.	and nevermore.
Wo ich ihn nicht hab,	Wherever I do not have him
Ist mir das Grab,	is for me the grave;
Die ganze Welt	the whole world
Ist mir vergällt.	is to me loathsome.
Mein armer Kopf	My poor head
Ist mir verrückt,	is deranged;
Mein armer Sinn	my poor mind
Ist mir zerstückt.	is shattered.
Nach ihm nur schau ich	For him only do I gaze
Zum Fenster hinaus,	out from the window;
Nach ihm nur geh ich	For him only do I go
Aus dem Haus.	out of the house.
Sein hoher Gang,	His fine gait,
Sein' edle Gestalt,	his noble stature,
Seines Mundes Lächeln,	his mouth's smile,
Seiner Augen Gewalt,	his eyes' power,
Und seiner Rede	and, of his speech,
Zauberfluss,	magic flow—
Sein Händedruck,	his handclasp,
Und ach, sein Kuss!	and, ah, his kiss!
Mein Busen drängt	My bosom yearns
Sich nach ihm hin,	for him;
Ach dürft' ich fassen	ah, could I embrace him
Und halten ihn,	and hold him,
Und küssen ihn,	and kiss him
So wie ich wollt',	as much as I wish,
An seinen Küssen	in his kisses
Vergehen sollt'.	I should perish.

mir___ das Grab, die gan - ze Welt___ ist___

mir___ ver - gällt. Mein ar - mer Kopf___ ist

mir___ ver - rückt,___ mein ar - mer Sinn___ ist

mir___ zer - stückt. Mei - ne

mehr. Mein Bu - sen drängt sich nach ihm hin, ach dürft' ich fas - sen und hal - ten ihn, und küs - sen

decresc.
p
cresc. poco a poco e accel.
f
ff

Gruppe aus dem Tartarus

poem by Johann Christoph Friedrich von Schiller

D 583. Original key. This song was composed in September of 1817, and published by Sauer and Leidesdorf as Opus 23, No. 1, in October of 1823. Schubert's first setting (D 396) of this poem, dated 1816, is only fourteen measures in length, and comprises just five lines of the poem. It's possible a second page, completing the autograph, is missing. In Greek mythology, "Tartarus" was a region beneath Hades used for confinement of the rebel Titans. It later came to mean Hades. In the *Illiad*, the damned look desperately "for a bridge over Cocytus, possibly regarding the river itself as a bridge to the world above, since it allegedly connects the world with Hades." Johannes Brahms arranged this song for male chorus and orchestra in 1862. Schiller (1759–1805), poet, playwright, essayist, and leading figure of German literature second only to his friend Goethe, was Schubert's source for forty-four songs, most of them composed in the earlier periods of Schubert's life. Schiller's lyrics were especially inspiring for the composer as an alternative to the strophic lied.

Gruppe aus dem Tartarus	Group in Tartarus
Horch—wie Murmeln des empörten Meeres,	Hark—like the murmuring of the aroused sea,
Wie durch hohler Felsen Becken weint ein Bach,	as through the basin of hollow rocks weeps a brook,
Stöhnt dort dumpfigtief ein schweres, leeres,	moans there, dankly deep, a heavy, hollow
Qualerpresstes Ach!	cry of woe wrung from the tormented ones.
Schmerz verzerret	Pain contorts
Ihr Gesicht. Verzweiflung sperret	their faces. Despair opens
Ihren Rachen fluchend auf.	their cursing jaws wide.
Hohl sind ihre Augen—ihre Blicke	Hollow are their eyes—their gazes
Spähen bang nach des Kozytus Brücke,	fix, fearfully, on Cocytus' bridge;
Folgen tränend seinem Trauerlauf.	they follow, weeping, its dreary course.
Fragen sich einander ängstlich leise,	They ask each other, softly anxious,
Ob noch nicht Vollendung sei?	if it not yet may be the end?
Ewigkeit schwingt über ihnen Kreise,	Eternity circles over them,
Bricht die Sense des Saturns entzwei.	breaks the scythe of Saturn in two.

Etwas geschwind

Herbst

poem by Ludwig Rellstab

D 945. Original key: E minor. This song was unknown until the 1890s, when an autograph was discovered in an album belonging to Heinrich Panofka, a violinist and acquaintance of Schubert. Dated April, 1828, it bears the inscription, "Zur freundlichen Erinnerung" [To cheerful memories]. It's uncertain why Schubert excluded it from his *Schwanengesang*. See "Liebesbotschaft" for notes on Rellstab and *Schwanengesang*.

Herbst

Es rauschen die Winde so herbstlich und kalt,
Verödet die Fluren, entblättert der Wald,
Ihr blumigen Auen, du sonniges Grün,
So welken die Blüten des Lebens dahin.

Es ziehen die Wolken so finster und grau,
Verschwunden die Sterne am himmlischen Blau.
Ach, wie die Gestirne am Himmel entfliehn,
So sinket die Hoffnung des Lebens dahin!

Ihr Tage des Lenzes, mit Rosen geschmückt,
Wo ich den Geliebten ans Herze gedrückt!
Kalt über den Hügel rauscht, Winde, dahin—
So sterben die Rosen des Lebens dahin!

Autumn

The winds roar so autumnal and cold;
bare the meadows, leafless the woods.
You flowery pastures, you sunny green—
so do the blossoms of life wither away.

The clouds pass so dark and grey;
vanished the stars in the heavenly blue.
Ah, as the stars flee from the sky
so does the hope of life give way.

You days of spring, with roses bedecked,
when I pressed my beloved to my heart!
Roar away coldly over the grave, winds!
So do the roses of life die away.

15
Le - bens_____ da - hin,_____ so
Le - bens_____ da - hin,_____ so
Le - bens_____ da - hin,_____ so

17
wel - ken die Blü - ten des Le -
sin - ket die Hoff - nung des Le -
ster - ben die Ro - sen des Le -

20
- bens da - hin.
- bens da - hin!
- bens da - hin!

Heidenröslein

poem by Johann Wolfgang von Goethe

D 257. Original key: G major. One of five Goethe songs written on August 19, 1815, this was published by Cappi and Diabelli as Opus 3, No. 3 in May, 1821. Three other Goethe settings ("Schäfers Klagelied," "Meeres Stille," and "Jägers Abendlied II") complete Opus 3, all dedicated "with great respect" to Ignaz von Mosel, assistant director of the court theaters in Vienna. See "An den Mond" for notes on Goethe.

Heidenröslein

Sah ein Knab ein Röslein stehn,
Röslein auf der Heiden,
War so jung und morgenschön,
Lief er schnell, es nah zu sehn,
Sah's mit vielen Freuden.
Röslein, Röslein, Röslein rot,
Röslein auf der Heiden.

Knabe sprach: ich breche dich,
Röslein auf der Heiden.
Röslein sprach: ich steche dich,
Dass du ewig denkst an mich,
Und ich will's nicht leiden.
Röslein, Röslein, Röslein rot,
Röslein auf der Heiden.

Und der wilde Knabe brach
's Röslein auf der Heiden;
Röslein wehrte sich und stach,
Half ihm doch kein Weh und Ach,
Musst' es eben leiden.
Röslein, Röslein, Röslein rot,
Röslein auf der Heiden.

Little Heath Rose

A lad saw a wild rose,
wild rose on the heath.
It was so young, and lovely as morning.
He ran quickly to look at it closely;
he looked at it with much joy.
Wild rose, wild rose, wild rose red,
wild rose on the heath.

The lad said, "I will pick you,
wild rose on the heath!"
The wild rose said, "I will prick you,
so that you will always remember me;
and I will not suffer from it."
Wild rose, wild rose, wild rose red,
wild rose on the heath.

And the impetuous lad picked
the wild rose on the heath.
The wild rose defended itself and pricked,
but grief and pain was of no avail;
it had to suffer after all.
Wild rose, wild rose, wild rose red,
wild rose on the heath.

Heliopolis I

poem by Johann Baptist Mayrhofer

D 753. Original key. The "Heliopolis" poems set by Schubert come from a collection dated 1821 and dedicated to Franz Schober. Written in April, 1822, the songs were published separately, "I" in November, 1826, as Opus 65, No. 3, and "II" in 1842, in Book 37 of *Nachlass* (See "Abendstern"). The sequence in the poetry collection had the first song as No. 5 and the second as No. 12, but the autograph version of Schubert's work indicated No. 12 for both songs. There is little doubt that Mayrhofer wrote the entire collection in hopes that Schubert would compose a complete cycle. See "Abendstern" for notes on Mayrhofer. See "An die Musik" for notes on Schober.

Heliopolis I

Im kalten, rauhen Norden
Ist Kunde mir geworden
Von einer Stadt, der Sonnenstadt;
Wo weilt das Schiff, wo ist der Pfad,
Die mich zu jenen Hallen tragen?
Von Menschen konnt' ich nichts erfragen,
Im Zwiespalt waren sie verworren.
Zur Blume, die sich Helios erkoren,
Die ewig in sein Antlitz blickt,
Wandt' ich mich nun und ward entzückt.

»Wende, so wie ich, zur Sonne
Deine Augen, dort ist Wonne,
Dort ist Leben;
Treu ergeben
Pilgre zu und zweifle nicht,
Ruhe findest du im Licht.
Licht erzeuget alle Gluten,
Hoffnungspflanzen, Tatenfluten!«

Heliopolis I

In the cold, harsh north,
news came to me
of a city—the city of sun.
Where tarries the ship, where is the path
that will take me to those halls?
From people could I ascertain nothing;
in discord were they entangled.
To the flower which Helios chose for himself,
which eternally gazes upon his countenance,
I then turned, and became enchanted.

"Turn, like me, to the sun
your eyes; there is rapture,
there is life.
Truly devoted,
pilgrimage onward and doubt not;
peace you will find in the light.
Light begets all passions—
hopes of people, torrents of achievements!"

in sein Ant - litz blickt, wandt' ich mich nun und ward __ ent - zückt.

»Wen - de, so wie ich, zur Son - ne dei - ne Au - gen,

dort ist Won - ne, dort ist Le - ben; treu er - ge - ben pil - gre __

zu und zweif - le __ nicht, Ru - he fin - dest du im Licht.

Heliopolis II

poem by Johann Baptist Mayrhofer

D 754. Original key. This song was originally composed for bass voice. The title of the poem, as part of the collection published in 1824, was "Im Hochgebirge" [On the Mountain Tops]. See "Abendstern" for notes on Mayrhofer. Also see "Heliopolis I."

Heliopolis II	Heliopolis II
Fels auf Felsen hingewälzet,	*Rock upon rock rolled,*
Fester Grund und treuer Halt:	*firm ground and steady footing,*
Wasserfälle, Windesschauer,	*waterfalls, wind's blasts,*
Unbegriffene Gewalt.	*uncomprehended power.*
Einsam auf Gebirges Zinne,	*Solitary on the mountain's pinnacle,*
Kloster wie auch Burgruine,	*cloister and castle ruins;*
Grab sie der Erinn'rung ein;	*engrave them in memory,*
Denn der Dichter lebt vom Sein.	*for the poet lives from being.*
Atme du den heil'gen Äther,	*Breathe the sacred ether;*
Schling die Arme um die Welt,	*entwine your arms around the world.*
Nur dem Würdigen, dem Großen	*Only with the worthy, the great*
Bleibe mutig zugesellt.	*stay bravely in company.*
Lass die Leidenschaften sausen	*Let the passions bluster*
Im metallenen Akkord,	*in strident chord;*
Wenn die starken Stürme brausen,	*when the violent storms rage,*
Findest du das rechte Wort.	*you will find the right word.*

blei - be mu - tig zu - ge - sellt.

cresc.

Lass die Lei - den - schaf - ten sau - sen

f   *fz*

im me - tal - le - nen Ak - kord, wenn die star - ken

Stür - me brau - sen, fin - dest du das rech - te, das rech - te

Im Abendrot

poem by Karl Lappe

D 799. Original key: A-flat major. Schubert set two Lappe poems, "Im Abendrot" and "Der Einsame," at about the same time, in February of 1825. The poems came from a collection published in 1824, *Lied und Leben* [Song and Life]. Lappe (1773–1843) was a poet and teacher in Pomerania.

Im Abendrot	At Sunset
Oh, wie schön ist deine Welt,	*Oh, how beautiful is your world,*
Vater, wenn sie golden strahlet,	*Father, when it shines golden,*
Wenn dein Glanz hernieder fällt,	*when your radiance descends*
Und den Staub mit Schimmer malet;	*and paints the dust with lustre,*
Wenn das Rot, das in der Wolke blinkt,	*when the red that gleams in the cloud*
In mein stilles Fenster sinkt.	*sinks into my quiet window.*
Könnt ich klagen, könnt ich zagen?	*Could I complain? Could I be faint-hearted,*
Irre sein an dir und mir?	*be mistaken about you and me?*
Nein, ich will im Busen tragen	*No, I will in my bosom carry*
Deinen Himmel schon allhier,	*your heaven wholly here;*
Und dies Herz, eh es zusammenbricht,	*and this heart, before it breaks,*
Trinkt noch Glut und schlürft noch Licht.	*shall still drink the glow and still savor the light.*

Sehr langsam, mit gehobener Dämpfung

Oh, wie schön ist dei - ne Welt, Va - ter, wenn sie gol - den

Hoffnung

poem by Johann Wolfgang von Goethe

D 295. Original key: F major. It's unknown when this song was written, despite two autographs, since neither is dated. Some historians think it was composed as early as 1815, while others believe it could have been as late as the fall of 1819. It was first published in 1872, by J.P. Gotthard, as No. 14 in a collection entitled *Forty Songs*. See "An den Mond" for notes on Goethe. Two other Schubert songs entitled "Hoffnung" are settings of a poem by Schiller.

Hoffnung

Schaff', das Tagwerk meiner Hände,
Hohes Glück, dass ich's vollende!
Lass, o lass mich nicht ermatten!
Nein, es sind nicht leere Träume:
Jetzt nur Stangen, diese Bäume
Geben einst noch Frucht und Schatten.

Hope

Provide the daily work of my hands,
sublime fortune, that I may complete it!
Let, oh let me not grow weary!
No, these are not idle dreams:
at present only shoots, these trees
will yet give, one day, fruit and shade.

Im Frühling

poem by Ernst Konrad Friedrich Schulze

D 882. Original key: G major. The poem comes from Schulze's *Poetisches Tagebuch* [Verse Journal], and was retitled by Schubert. The first version was written in March, 1826, with *Langsam* [Slow] as the tempo marking. It was first published in the *Weiner Zeitschrift für Kunst, Literatur, Theater und Mode* in September of 1828. Later that year it appeared as the first of the four songs in Opus 101, and in 1835 it was published in Book 25 of *Nachlass* (See "Abendstern"). See "Auf der Bruck" for notes on Schulze.

Im Frühling	In the Springtime
Still sitz ich an des Hügels Hang,	*Quietly I sit on the hillside.*
Der Himmel ist so klar,	*The sky is so clear.*
Das Lüftchen spielt im grünen Tal,	*The zephyr plays in the green valley*
Wo ich, beim ersten Frühlingsstrahl,	*where I, in the first rays of springtime*
Einst, ach, so glücklich war;	*once, alas, was so happy,*
Wo ich an ihrer Seite ging	*where I at her side walked*
So traulich und so nah,	*so intimately and so close,*
Und tief im dunkeln Felsenquell	*and deep in the dark rock's spring*
Den schönen Himmel blau und hell	*saw the beautiful heavens, blue and bright,*
Und sie im Himmel sah.	*and saw her in the heavens.*
Sieh, wie der bunte Frühling schon	*See how the colorful springtime already*
Aus Knosp' und Blüte blickt,	*appears from bud and blossom!*
Nicht alle Blüten sind mir gleich,	*Not all blossoms are the same to me;*
Am liebsten pflückt' ich von dem Zweig,	*I like best to pick from the branch*
Von welchem sie gepflückt.	*from which she picked.*
Denn alles ist wie damals noch,	*For all is still as it was in those days:*
Die Blumen, das Gefild;	*the flowers, the fields;*
Die Sonne scheint nicht minder hell,	*the sun shines no less brightly,*
Nicht minder freundlich schwimmt im Quell	*no less cheerfully floats in the spring*
Das blaue Himmelsbild.	*the blue heavens' image.*
Es wandeln nur sich Will' und Wahn,	*Only will and illusion change;*
Es wechseln Lust und Streit,	*pleasure alternates with strife.*
Vorüber flieht der Liebe Glück,	*Away flies love's happiness,*
Und nur die Liebe bleibt zurück,	*and only the love remains behind—*
Die Lieb' und ach, das Leid.	*the love and, alas, the sorrow.*
O wär ich doch ein Vöglein nur	*Oh, were I but only a little bird*
Dort an dem Wiesenhang,	*there on the meadow's slope;*
Dann blieb ich auf den Zweigen hier	*then I would stay in the branches here*
Und säng ein süßes Lied von ihr	*and sing a sweet song about her*
Den ganzen Sommer lang.	*all summer long.*

Still sitz ich an des Hü - gels Hang, der Him-mel ist so klar, das

Lüft-chen spielt im grü - nen Tal, wo ich, beim ers-ten Früh-lings-strahl, einst, ach, so glück-lich war, so glück-lich

ppp   cresc.   p

war;   wo ich an ih - rer Sei - te ging so trau-lich und so nah, und

pp

tief im dun-keln Fel - sen-quell den schö - nen Him-mel blau und hell und sie im Him-mel sah, und

fp   pp

sie_ im_ Him-mel sah.

Sieh, wie der bun - te Früh - ling schon aus

Knosp' und Blü - te__ blickt, Nicht al - le__ Blü - ten__ sind mir gleich, am

liebs - ten pflückt' ich von dem Zweig, von wel - chem sie ge-pflückt, von wel-chem sie ge-

pflückt.   Denn al - les ist wie da - mals noch, die Blu-men, das Ge-fild;   die

Son - ne scheint nicht min - der hell, nicht min - der freund-lich schwimmt im Quell das

cresc.

blau - e Him - mels - bild,   das— blau-e— Him - mels - bild.

pp

Es

mf   *p*

an dem Wie - sen - hang, dann blieb ich auf den Zwei - gen hier und

säng ein sü - ßes_ Lied von ihr den gan - zen Som - mer lang, den_

cresc.

pp

gan - zen_ Som - mer_ lang, ich säng von ihr

ppp

den gan - zen Som - mer_ lang.

Im Haine

poem by Franz Ritter von Bruchmann

D 738. Original key A major. Though the autograph is missing, it's likely that Schubert wrote this song in the winter of 1822, using a manuscript copy of the poem. The song was published by A.W. Pennauer in July, 1826, as Op. 56, No. 3, and dedicated to Karl Pinterics. An Italian translation was added in the second edition, probably by Jacob Craigher. See "Am See" for notes on Bruchmann. See "Die junge Nonne" for notes on Craigher.

Im Haine	In the Grove
Sonnenstrahlen	*Sunbeams*
Durch die Tannen,	*through the pines,*
Wie sie fallen,	*as they fall,*
Ziehn von dannen	*draw from thence*
Alle Schmerzen,	*all sorrows;*
Und im Herzen	*and in hearts*
Wohnet reiner Friede nur.	*dwells only pure tranquillity.*
Stilles Sausen	*Hushed blowing*
Lauer Lüfte,	*of balmy breezes*
Und im Brausen	*and, in their effervescence,*
Zarte Düfte,	*sweet fragrances*
Die sich neigen	*which float down*
Aus den Zweigen,	*from the branches,*
Atmet aus die ganze Flur.	*breathe from the whole meadow.*
Wenn nur immer	*If only, forever,*
Dunkle Bäume,	*dark trees,*
Sonnenschimmer,	*sun's shimmer,*
Grüne Säume	*green forests' edges*
Uns umblühten	*were to bloom around us*
Und umglühten,	*and glow around us,*
Tilgend aller Qualen Spur.	*obliterating all trace of afflictions.*

Son - nen - strah - len durch die Tan - nen, wie_ sie fal - len, ziehn von
Stil - les Sau - sen lau - er Lüf - te, und_ im Brau - sen zar - te
Wenn nur im - mer dunk - le Bäu - me, Son - nen - schim - mer, grü - ne

Im Walde

poem by Karl Wilhelm Friedrich von Schlegel

D 708. Original key: E major. The autograph of this song is dated December, 1820. When it was published, in 1832, in book 16 of *Nachlass* (See "Abendstern"), Diabelli changed its key to E-flat and its title to "Waldesnacht," possibly to avoid confusion with Schubert's setting of Schulze's "Im Walde," published in 1828. Schlegel (1772–1829) was the poet for 16 of Schubert's songs, most of which date from 1819–1822. After an early and unsuccessful stint at banking, he was a university student, eventually co-founding *Das Athenaeum* with his brother, August Wilhelm von Schlegel (also a source for Schubert's settings). He married and moved to Vienna, took a position in government service there and converted to Roman Catholicism. In Vienna, Schlegel was part of a group of writers and philosophers which included many of the Schubert circle, including Franz von Bruchmann. See "Am See" for notes on Bruchmann. See "Ständchen" for notes on A.W. von Schlegel.

Im Walde	In the Forest
Windes Rauschen, Gottes Flügel,	Wind's rustle, God's wings,
Tief in kühler Waldesnacht,	deep in the cool forest night;
Wie der Held in Rosses Bügel,	as the hero into his horse's stirrups,
Schwingt sich des Gedankens Macht.	leaps the power of thought.
Wie die alten Tannen sausen,	As the old pines rustle,
Hört man Geisteswogen brausen,	one hears waves of the spirit roar.
Herrlich ist der Flamme Leuchten	Glorious is the flame's glow
In des Morgenglanzes Rot,	in the morning splendor's red,
Oder die das Feld beleuchten,	or the lightning which illuminates the field,
Blitze, schwanger oft von Tod.	pregnant often with death.
Rasch die Flamme zuckt und lodert,	Quickly the flame flashes and burns,
Wie zu Gott hinauf gefodert.	as if summoned upward to God.
Ewig's Rauschen sanfter Quellen	Eternally the murmur of gentle springs
Zaubert Blumen aus dem Schmerz,	charms flowers away from their sorrow;
Trauer doch in linden Wellen	yet grief, in soft waves,
Schlägt uns lockend an das Herz;	beats alluringly upon our hearts.
Fernab hin der Geist gezogen,	Far away is the spirit borne
Die uns locken, durch die Wogen.	on the billows which lure us.
Drang des Lebens aus der Hülle,	Craving of life to be free from impediment,
Kampf der starken Triebe wild,	struggle against strong, wild urges
Wird zur schönsten Liebesfülle,	become, through the breath of the spirit,
Durch des Geistes Hauch gestillt.	quieted in the most beautiful fullness of love.
Schöpferischer Lüfte Wehen	The fluttering of creative breezes
Fühlt man durch die Seele gehen.	ones feels go through the soul.
Windes Rauschen, Gottes Flügel,	Wind's rustle, God's wings,
Tief in dunkler Waldesnacht,	deep in the dark forest night;
Frei gegeben alle Zügel,	freed from all restraints,
Schwingt sich des Gedankens Macht.	the power of thought soars.
Hört in Lüften ohne Grausen	One hears in the breezes, without dread,
Den Gesang der Geister brausen.	the song of the spirit roar.

lo - dert, wie zu Gott hin - auf ge -

fo - dert.

E - wig's Rau - schen

sanf - ter Quel - len zau - bert Blu - men aus dem Schmerz,

stillt. Schöp - fe - ri - scher Lüf - te We - hen

fühlt man durch die See - le ge - hen,

schöp - fe - ri - scher Lüf - te We - hen fühlt man durch die

See - le ge - hen, fühlt man

Jägers Abendlied

poem by Johann Wolfgang von Goethe

D 368. Original key: D-flat major. There is no autograph of this song, but the copy that Schubert made for Goethe and sent to him in 1816, and which excluded the third of four verses, is now in Berlin. That version was published in 1821 as Opus 3, No. 4, by Cappi and Diabelli. Opus 3 included three additional Goethe settings (See "Heidenröslein"). A version of the song in the Witteczek-Spaun collection has vocal ornamentation by Vogl, who routinely embellished Schubert's songs in performance. Schubert disregarded Goethe's instructions that, "the first and third verses have to be recited energetically, with some fire while the second and fourth must be more gentle, because here a new emotion has appeared." See "An den Mond" for notes on Goethe. See "Ganymed" for notes on Vogl.

Jägers Abendlied

Im Felde schleich ich still und wild,
Gespannt mein Feuerrohr,
Da schwebt so licht dein liebes Bild,
Dein süßes Bild mir vor.

Du wandelst jetzt wohl still und mild
Durch Feld und liebes Tal,
Und ach, mein schnell verrauschend Bild,
Stellt sich dir's nicht einmal?

Mir ist es, denk ich nur an dich,
Als in den Mond zu sehn,
Ein stiller Friede kommt auf mich,
Weiß nicht, wie mir geschehn.

Huntsman's Evening Song

In the fields I prowl, silent and fierce,
cocked my musket;
then hovers so clearly your beloved image,
your sweet image, before me.

You are perhaps walking now, silent and gentle,
through field and dear valley;
and ah, my sudden fleeting image—
does it ever appear to you?

I feel, when I think only of you,
as though I am gazing at the moon.
A silent peace comes over me;
I know not how it happens.

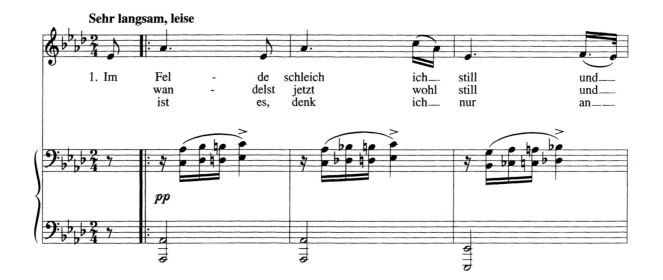

Klaglied

poem by Johann Friedrich Rochlitz

D 23. Original key: G minor. The early composition date, 1812, has made some historians believe that this could have been Schubert's first song. It is without question the first complete strophic song composed by him, and is one of only three songs to the poetry of Rochlitz. It was published in November, 1830, by Josef Czerny, in a group of three songs, later designated Opus 131. See "An die Laute" for notes on Rochlitz.

Klaglied	*Lamentation*
Meine Ruh ist dahin,	*My peace is gone,*
Meine Freud ist entflohn,	*my joy has fled;*
In dem Säuseln der Lüfte,	*in the rustling of the breezes,*
In dem Murmeln des Bachs	*in the murmuring of the brook*
Hör ich bebend nur Klageton.	*I hear, trembling, only plaintive sound.*
Seinem schmeichelnden Wort	*His flattering word*
Und dem Druck seiner Hand,	*and the press of his hand,*
Seinem heißen Verlangen,	*his passionate desire,*
Seinem glühenden Kuss,	*his burning kiss,*
Weh mir, dass ich nicht widerstand.	*woe is me, that I did not resist.*
Wenn ich von fern ihn seh,	*When I see him from afar*
Will ich ihn zu mir ziehn;	*I want to draw him to me;*
Kaum entdeckt mich sein Auge,	*no sooner does his eye discern me,*
Kaum tritt näher er mir,	*no sooner does he come closer to me,*
Möcht' ich gern in mein Grab entfliehn.	*than I would gladly escape to my grave.*
Einmal, ach, einmal nur	*Once, ah, only once*
Möcht ich ihn glücklich sehn	*could I see him happy*
Hier am klopfenden Herzen,	*here upon my throbbing heart,*
An der sehnenden Brust:	*upon my longing breast:*
Wollte lächelnd dann untergehn!	*would I then perish smiling!*

Kla - - - ge - ton, hör ich nur Kla - - ge - ton.
wi - - - der - stand, dass ich nicht wi - - der - stand.

Wenn ich von fern ihn seh, will ich ihn zu mir
Ein - mal, ach, ein - mal nur möcht ich ihn glück - lich

ziehn, wenn ich von fern ihn seh, will ich ihn zu mir ziehn; kaum ent-
sehn, ein - mal, ach, ein - mal nur möcht ich ihn glück-lich sehn hier am

28

deckt_____ mich sein Au - ge,   kaum tritt nä - _____ her er
klop - _____ fen - den Her - zen,   an der seh - _____ nen-den

pp

31

mir,_____   möcht   ich   gern in   mein
Brust:_____   woll - te   lä - chelnd   dann

34

Grab_____   ent - fliehn,   gern in mein Grab_____   ent - er
un - _____   ter - gehn,   lä - chelnd dann un - _____   ter -

fp

37

fliehn.
gehn!

ppp

Lachen und Weinen

poem by Friedrich Rückert

D 777. Original key: A-flat major. The poem is from a collection of poetry, *Östliche Rosen* [Oriental Roses], published near the end of 1821, and only later, in 1837, given the title "Lachens und Weinens Grund" [The Reason for Laughter and Weeping] by the poet. "Lachen und Weinen" is Schubert's own title. The summer of 1822 is the best approximation of its date of origin. It was published, alongside two other Rückert settings and one Platen setting, as Op. 59, No. 4, by Sauer and Leidesdorf, in September of 1826. See "Dass sie hier gewesen!" for notes on Rückert and *Östliche Rosen*. Also see "Du bist die Ruh" and "Du liebst mich nicht."

Lachen und Weinen	*Laughter and Weeping*
Lachen und Weinen zu jeglicher Stunde	*Laughter and weeping, at whatever hour,*
Ruht bei der Lieb auf so mancherlei Grunde.	*are based, in the case of love, on so many different reasons.*
Morgens lacht' ich vor Lust;	*Every morning I laughed for joy;*
Und warum ich nun weine	*and why I now weep*
Bei des Abendes Scheine,	*in the evening's glow*
Ist mir selb' nicht bewusst.	*is even to myself unknown.*
Weinen und Lachen zu jeglicher Stunde	*Weeping and laughter, at whatever hour,*
Ruht bei der Lieb auf so mancherlei Grunde.	*are based, in the case of love, on so many different reasons.*
Abends weint' ich vor Schmerz;	*Evenings I have wept for sorrow;*
Und warum du erwachen	*and how can you wake up*
Kannst am Morgen mit Lachen,	*in the morning with laughter,*
Muss ich dich fragen, o Herz.	*must I ask you, oh heart.*

307

wusst.

Wei - nen und La - chen zu jeg - li - cher Stun - de ruht_ bei der

Lieb_ auf so man - cher-lei Grun - de. A - bends weint' ich vor

Schmerz; und wa - rum du er - wa - chen kannst am Mor - gen mit

cresc.

La - chen, muss ich dich fra - gen, o Herz, muss ich dich fra - gen, o

Herz.

pp

Liebe schwärmt auf allen Wegen

poem by Johann Wolfgang von Goethe

D 239. Original key: D major. This "Ariette" (as described in the original score) is from Schubert's singspiel *Claudine von Villa Bella*. It is sung by Claudine in Act I, the only surviving act from the stage work. See "An den Mond" for notes on Goethe.

Liebe schwärmt auf allen Wegen	*Love Revels on All Paths*
Liebe schwärmt auf allen Wegen;	*Love revels on all paths;*
Treue wohnt für sich allein.	*fidelity lives for itself alone.*
Liebe kommt euch rasch entgegen;	*Love will come swiftly to you;*
Aufgesucht will Treue sein.	*sought after will fidelity be.*

Lie - be kommt euch rasch ent - ge - gen;

auf - ge - sucht will__ Treu - e sein.

Lie - be schwärmt auf al - len We - gen;

Treu - e wohnt für__ sich al - lein.__

cresc.

Lied der Mignon (Heiß mich nicht reden)

poem by Johann Wolfgang von Goethe

D 877, No. 2. Original key: E minor. There are two versions of this song: D 726, in B minor, was composed in April, 1821. This version was composed in January of 1826. Published by Diabelli in March, 1827, as Op. 62, No. 2, this song and three others comprised "Songs from *Wilhelm Meister* by Goethe," and was dedicated to Mathilde, Princess Schwarzenberg. The poem's title is "Mignon," which Schubert chose for the first version, but he named the second version "Lied der Mignon." See "An den Mond" for notes on Goethe. See "Mignons Gesang (Kennst du das Land)" for notes on Mignon and *Wilhelm Meister*.

Lied der Mignon (Heiß mich nicht reden)	*Mignon's Song* *(Bid Me Not Speak)*
Heiß mich nicht reden, heiß mich schweigen, Denn mein Geheimnis ist mir Pflicht; Ich möchte dir mein ganzes Innre zeigen, Allein das Schicksal will es nicht.	*Bid me not speak; bid me to keep silent,* *for my secret is my duty.* *I would like to show you my whole soul,* *but fate wills it not.*
Zur rechten Zeit vertreibt der Sonne Lauf Die finstre Nacht, und sie muss sich erhellen, Der harte Fels schließt seinen Busen auf, Missgönnt der Erde nicht die tief verborgnen Quellen.	*In good time the sun's course will dispel* *the dark night, and it must brighten;* *the hard rock will unlock its bosom,* *will not begrudge the earth's deeply concealed springs.*
Ein jeder sucht im Arm des Freundes Ruh, Dort kann die Brust in Klagen sich ergießen. Allein ein Schwur drückt mir die Lippen zu, Und nur ein Gott vermag sie aufzuschließen.	*Every person seeks rest in the arms of a friend;* *there can the heart in lament pour forth.* *But an oath seals my lips,* *and only a god can open them.*

Ein je - der sucht im Arm des Freun-des Ruh, dort kann die Brust in

pp

Kla-gen sich er-gie-ßen, in Kla - gen sich er - gie - ßen. Al - lein ein Schwur drückt mir die Lip-pen

cresc.

zu, und nur ein Gott ver-mag sie auf-zu-schlie - ßen, ein Schwur drückt mir die Lip-pen

fz *p* *cresc.*

zu, und nur ein Gott, ein Gott ver-mag sie auf-zu-schlie - ßen.

f *ff* *ffz* *p*

Lied der Mignon (So lasst mich scheinen)

poem by Johann Wolfgang von Goethe

D 877, No. 3. Original key: B major. Goethe wrote this poem in 1796 for the ending of his novel *Wilhelm Meister*, at the death of Mignon. Mignon is ill, and having recently dressed up as an angel for a party, she begs permission to continue wearing her costume. She then sings this song. Schubert made four attempts at setting this poem. The first two exist only as fragments, and the third, D 727, in B minor, is rarely heard. Schubert composed this setting in January, 1826, and it was published by Diabelli as Opus 62, No. 3, in March of 1827. Schubert altered the text in the last line of the first verse from "feste Haus" [solid, permanent dwelling place] to "dunkle Haus" [dark dwelling place]. See "An den Mond" for notes on Goethe. See "Mignons Gesang (Kennst du das Land)" for notes on Mignon and *Wilhelm Meister*.

Lied der Mignon
(So lasst mich scheinen)

So lasst mich scheinen, bis ich werde,
Zieht mir das weiße Kleid nicht aus,
Ich eile von der schönen Erde
Hinab in jenes dunkle Haus.

Dort ruh ich eine kleine Stille,
Dann öffnet sich der frische Blick,
Ich lasse dann die reine Hülle,
Den Gürtel und den Kranz zurück.

Und jene himmlischen Gestalten,
Sie fragen nicht nach Mann und Weib,
Und keine Kleider, keine Falten
Umgeben den verklärten Leib.

Zwar lebt' ich ohne Sorg und Mühe,
Doch fühlt' ich tiefen Schmerz genung,
Vor Kummer altert' ich zu frühe,
Macht mich auf ewig wieder jung.

Mignon's Song
(So Let Me Seem)

So let me seem, until I so become;
do not take off my white robe!
I shall hasten from the beautiful earth
down to that dark dwelling place.

There shall I rest in a brief silence;
then my refreshed eyes will open.
I will then leave the chaste raiment,
the sash and the wreath behind.

And those heavenly forms
question not if one is man or woman;
and no garments, no folds
enclose the transfigured body.

True, I lived without care and trouble;
yet I felt deep pain enough.
From grief I aged too early;
make me forever again young!

von der schö-nen Er - de hin-ab in je - nes dunk-le__ Haus.

Dort ruh ich ei - ne klei - ne Stil - le, dann öff - net sich der fri - sche

Blick, ich las - se dann die rei - ne__ Hül - le, den Gür - tel und den Kranz zu-rück.

Und je - ne himm - li-schen Ge - stal - ten, sie fra - gen nicht nach Mann und

Weib, und kei-ne Klei - der, kei - ne Fal - ten um-ge-ben den ver - klär - ten_ Leib.

Zwar lebt' ich oh - ne Sorg und Mü - he, doch fühlt' ich

tie-fen Schmerz_ ge-nung, vor Kum-mer al - tert' ich zu_ frü - he, macht mich auf

e - wig, auf e - wig wie-der jung.

Lied der Mignon (Nur wer die Sehnsucht kennt)

poem by Johann Wolfgang von Goethe

D 877, No. 4. Original key: A minor. Schubert set this poem six times, including four solo settings, one duet and one quintet for men, naming them variously, "Lied der Mignon," "Die Sehnsucht," "Mignons Gesang," or simply, "Mignon." Schubert's duet version was published as part of the same opus as this setting. The text comes from the end of Book 4 of Goethe's novel *Wilhelm Meister*, a duet between Mignon and the Harper, though in an earlier version of the novel Mignon sings alone. Composed in January, 1826, this song was published by Diabelli in March, 1827, as Opus 62, No. 4. Schubert used a revised version of "Ins stille Land," written in 1816, as a basis for its composition. See "An den Mond" for notes on Goethe. See "Mignons Gesang (Kennst du das Land)" for notes on Mignon and *Wilhelm Meister*.

Lied der Mignon	*Mignon's Song*
(Nur wer die Sehnsucht kennt)	*(Only he who knows longing)*
Nur wer die Sehnsucht kennt,	*Only he who knows longing*
Weiß, was ich leide.	*knows what I suffer.*
Allein und abgetrennt	*Alone and separated*
Von aller Freude,	*from all joy,*
Seh ich ans Firmament	*I look to the firmament*
Nach jener Seite.	*toward yonder direction.*
Ach, der mich liebt und kennt,	*Ah, he who loves and knows me*
Ist in der Weite.	*is far away.*
Es schwindelte mir, es brennt	*I am reeling; on fire are*
Mein Eingeweide.	*my vitals.*

Meeres Stille

poem by Johann Wolfgang von Goethe

D 216. Original key. There are two versions of this song, composed respectively on June 20 and 21, 1815. The poem and its companion piece, "Glückliche Fahrt" [Prosperous Journey], come from an experience Goethe had while traveling by boat from Naples to Sicily, a trip marked by dramatic changes in the weather. This is the second of the two versions, and was published by Diabelli in May, 1821, as Opus 3, No. 2, with a dedication to Ignaz von Mosel (See "Heidenröslein"). See "An den Mond" for notes on Goethe.

Meeres Stille	Sea Stillness
Tiefe Stille herrscht im Wasser,	*Deep stillness reigns in the water;*
Ohne Regung ruht das Meer,	*without motion rests the sea.*
Und bekümmert sieht der Schiffer	*And, troubled, the sailor looks at*
Glatte Fläche rings umher.	*the smooth surface all around.*
Keine Luft von keiner Seite!	*No breeze from any direction!*
Todesstille fürchterlich!	*Dead calm—terrifying!*
In der ungeheuern Weite	*In the enormous expanse*
Reget keine Welle sich.	*stirs not a wave.*

sieht der Schif-fer glat-te Flä-che rings um-her.

Kei-ne Luft von kei-ner Sei-te! To-des-

stil-le fürch-ter-lich! In der un-ge-

heu-ern Wei-te re-get kei-ne Wel-le sich.

Memnon

poem by Johann Baptist Mayrhofer

D 541. Original key. Memnon was the son of Eos, the Dawn. When he went to assist Priam, he was slain by Achilles. A statue of Amenophis was called Memnon by the Greeks. When struck by the sun's rays, the statue was believed to have made the sound of a plucked chord. Written in March, 1817, the song was published by Cappi and Diabelli as Opus 6, No. 1, in August of 1821. Schubert dedicated the song to Johann Michael Vogl. "Memnon" was orchestrated by Brahms in 1862. See "Abendstern" for notes on Mayrhofer. See "Ganymed" for notes on Vogl.

Memnon

Den Tag hindurch nur einmal mag ich sprechen,
Gewohnt zu schweigen immer und zu trauern,
Wenn durch die nachtgebornen Nebelmauern
Aurorens Purpurstrahlen liebend brechen.

Für Menschenohren sind es Harmonien.
Weil ich die Klage selbst melodisch künde,
Und durch der Dichtung Glut das Rauhe ründe,
Vermuten sie in mir ein selig Blühen.

In mir, nach dem des Todes Arme langen,
In dessen tiefstem Herzen Schlangen wühlen,
Genährt von meinen schmerzlichen Gefühlen,
Fast wütend durch ein ungestillt Verlangen:

Mit dir, des Morgens Göttin, mich zu einen,
Und weit von diesem nichtigen Getriebe,
Aus Sphären edler Freiheit, aus Sphären reiner Liebe,
Ein stiller bleicher Stern herab zu scheinen.

Memnon

Throughout the day only once am I permitted to speak,
accustomed to being ever silent, and to grieving:
when, through the night-born walls of mist,
Aurora's crimson rays lovingly break through.

For men's ears it is harmony.
Since I proclaim my lament melodically,
and through the ardor of poetry soften its harshness,
they imagine within me a happy bloom.

Within me, to whom the arms of death reach out,
in whose heart's depths serpents gnaw,
nourished by my anguished feelings,
almost gone mad from an unappeased longing:

With you, goddess of morning, to be united,
and, far from this futile bustle,
from spheres of noble freedom, from spheres of pure love
to shine down as a silent, pale star.

wohnt zu schwei-gen im-mer und zu trau-ern, wenn durch die nacht-ge-bor-nen

Ne - bel-mau - ern Au - ro-rens Pur-pur-strah - len lie - bend bre -

chen. Für Men-schen-

oh - ren sind es Har - mo - ni - en. Weil ich die Kla - ge selbst me-lo - disch

Litanei

poem by Johann Georg Jacobi

D 343. Original key. The complete title for this nine-verse litany, composed in August, 1816, is "Auf das Fest aller Seelen" [For the Feast of All Souls]. The autograph, with just the first verse, a repeat sign and the title "Am Tage aller Seelen," is in the Grob album (See "Am Grabe Anselmos"). We have included the complete poem for comprehension. A singer may choose to perform additional verses. The tempo marking is *Langsam mit Andacht* [Slow, with devotion] and there is no piano introduction. The song was published in 1831, in Book 10 of *Nachlass* (See "Abendstern"). It's interesting to note, that in a diary entry just two months prior to the creation of this song, Schubert recorded some thoughts about his deceased mother that had come to him while strolling through a local cemetery. Jacobi (1740–1814) was a poet, editor and professor of philosophy at Halle and Freiberg. His poems were published in 1816 and Schubert's seven settings are from August and September of that year.

Litanei

Ruhn in Frieden alle Seelen,
Die vollbracht ein banges Quälen,
Die vollendet süßen Traum,
Lebenssatt, geboren kaum,
Aus der Welt hinüber schieden:
Alle Seelen ruhn in Frieden!

Die sich hier Gespielen suchten,
Öfter weinten, nimmer fluchten,
Wenn von ihrer treuen Hand
Keiner je den Druck verstand:
Alle, die von hinnen schieden,
Alle Seelen ruhn in Frieden!

Liebevoller Mädchen Seelen,
Deren Tränen nicht zu zählen,
Die ein falscher Freund verließ,
Und die blinde Welt verstieß:
Alle, die von hinnen schieden,
Alle Seelen ruhn in Frieden!

Und der Jüngling, dem, verborgen,
Seine Braut am frühen Morgen,
Weil ihn Lieb' ins Grab gelegt,
Auf sein Grab die Kerze trägt:
Alle, die von hinnen schieden,
Alle Seelen ruhn in Frieden!

Alle Geister, die, voll Klarheit,
Wurden Märtyrer der Wahrheit,
Kämpften für das Heiligtum,
Suchten nicht der Marter Ruhm:
Alle, die von hinnen schieden,
Alle Seelen ruhn in Frieden!

Und die nie der Sonne lachten,
Unterm Mond auf Dornen wachten,
Gott, im reinen Himmelslicht
Einst zu sehn von Angesicht:
Alle, die von hinnen schieden,
Alle Seelen ruhn in Frieden!

Litany

May all souls rest in peace—
those who have done with an anxious torment,
those who have consummated a sweet dream,
satiated with life, scarcely born,
from the world departed:
All souls rest in peace!

They who sought companions here,
often wept, never cursed
when from their sincere hand
no one ever understood the grasp:
All who have departed from here—
all souls rest in peace!

The souls of loving maidens,
whose tears are not to be numbered,
whom a false friend abandoned
and the blind world rejected:
All who have departed from here—
all souls rest in peace!

And the young man, for whom clandestinely
his bride, in the early morning
as she lovingly laid him in the grave,
bore the candle to his grave:
All who have departed from here—
all souls rest in peace!

All spirits which, full of lucidity,
became martyrs for the truth,
fought for the shrine,
sought not the martyr's glory:
All who have departed from here—
all souls rest in peace!

And they upon whom the sun never smiled,
who beneath the moon lay awake upon thorns
that God, in the pure light of heaven,
one day they may see face to face:
All who have departed from here—
all souls rest in peace!

Und die gern im Rosengarten	And they who gladly in the rose garden
Bei dem Freudenbecher harrten,	at the cup of joy tarried
Aber dann, zur bösen Zeit,	but then, in hard times,
Schmeckten seine Bitterkeit:	tasted its bitterness:
Alle, die von hinnen schieden,	All who have departed from here—
Alle Seelen ruhn in Frieden!	all souls rest in peace!
Auch die keinen Frieden kannten,	Also, they who knew no peace,
Aber Mut und Stärke sandten	but whom courage and strength sent
Über leichenvolles Feld	over the corpse-strewn battlefield
In die halbentschlafne Welt:	in the half-deceased world:
Alle, die von hinnen schieden,	All who have departed from here—
Alle Seelen ruhn in Frieden!	all souls rest in peace!
Ruhn in Frieden alle Seelen,	May all souls rest in peace—
Die vollbracht ein banges Quälen,	those who have done with an anxious torment,
Die vollendet süßen Traum,	those who have consummated a sweet dream,
Lebenssatt, geboren kaum,	satiated with life, scarcely born,
Aus der Welt hinüber schieden:	from the world departed:
Alle Seelen ruhn in Frieden!	All souls rest in peace!

Mignons Gesang (Kennst du das Land?)

poem by Johann Wolfgang von Goethe

D 321. Original key: A major (transposed to F major for the first edition). This poem comes from Book 3 of Goethe's novel, *Wilhelm Meister*. Mignon, a character with a colorful past, the particulars of which are not known until the end of the novel, is the daughter of Harper by his demented sister, Sperata. She's taken from her incestuous mother to be raised by foster parents in the woods near a lake. One day, while wandering the countryside, she's kidnapped by a circus troupe, taken to Germany, and is there discovered by Wilhelm, who purchases her freedom. In this song Mignon addresses Wilhelm first as her lover and then, later, as her protector and father. The song was composed on October 23, 1815, and published in December, 1832, in Book 20 of *Nachlass* (See "Abendstern"). Schubert's setting of "Kennst du das Land" was written after Beethoven's and is in the same key. It's believed that Schubert, due to his sensitivity to the inevitable comparisons, kept the song from publication in his lifetime. The Mignon songs are untitled, so they are usually designated by their first lines. See "An den Mond" for notes on Goethe.

Mignons Gesang (Kennst du das Land?)	Mignon's Song (*Do You Know the Land?*)
Kennst du das Land, wo die Zitronen blühn,	*Do you know the land where the lemons blossom,*
Im dunklen Laub die Goldorangen glühn,	*midst dark leaves the golden oranges glow,*
Ein sanfter Wind vom blauen Himmel weht,	*a soft wind from the blue heaven blows,*
Die Myrte still und hoch der Lorbeer steht,	*the myrtle is still and the laurel tall?*
Kennst du es wohl?	*Do you know it?*
Dahin! dahin	*There! There*
Möcht ich mit dir, o mein Geliebter, ziehn!	*would I go with you, oh my beloved!*
Kennst du das Haus? Auf Säulen ruht sein Dach,	*Do you know the house? On pillars rests its roof;*
Es glänzt der Saal, es schimmert das Gemach,	*the hall gleams, the room shines,*
Und Marmorbilder stehn und sehn mich an:	*and marble statues stand and look at me:*
Was hat man dir, du armes Kind, getan?	*What have they done to you, you poor child?*
Kennst du es wohl?	*Do you know it?*
Dahin! dahin	*There! There*
Möcht ich mit dir, o mein Beschützer, ziehn!	*would I go with you, oh my protector!*
Kennst du den Berg und seinen Wolkensteg?	*Do you know the mountain and its clouded path?*
Das Maultier sucht im Nebel seinen Weg;	*The mule seeks, in the mist, its way.*
In Höhlen wohnt der Drachen alte Brut;	*In caves dwells the ancient brood of dragons;*
Es stürzt der Fels und über ihn die Flut,	*the rock plunges down, and over it the torrent.*
Kennst du ihn wohl?	*Do you know it?*
Dahin! dahin	*There! There*
Geht unser Weg! o Vater, lass uns ziehn.	*leads our way! Oh father, let us go!*

Brut; es stürzt der Fels und ü - ber ihn die Flut,

kennst — du ihn wohl?

Da - hin, da -

hin! — da - hin geht un - ser Weg! o Va - ter, lass uns

Etwas geschwinder

Nacht und Träume

poem by Matthäus von Collin

D 827. Original key: B major. Like the other Collin settings, this was written in late 1822 or early 1823, and certainly prior to June of 1823, when it was heard by Josef von Spaun at St. Florian. Schubert created his setting from a manuscript copy of the poem, which wasn't published until 1827. The original publication, Opus 43, No. 2, from July of 1825, mistakenly named Schiller as the poet. A slightly different version, part of the Spaun family collection, is marked *Langsam, Sempre legato* [Slow, Always legato]. Spaun (1788–1865) was a distinguished government official and the first to recognize Schubert's genius. It was through him that Schubert came to know Mayrhofer, Vogl, Schober and Witteczek, all of whom were important to Schubert's growth as a composer and musician, and it was Spaun's idea to have Schubert's songs published in a series of volumes arranged by poet. Spaun's *Memoirs* contains a number of important biographical accounts of Schubert. See "Der Zwerg" for notes on Collin.

Nacht und Träume	Night and Dreams
Heil'ge Nacht, du sinkest nieder!	*Hallowed night, you sink down!*
Nieder wallen auch die Träume,	*Downward float also the dreams,*
Wie dein Mondlicht durch die Räume,	*like your moonlight, through space,*
Durch der Menschen stille Brust.	*through the silent bosom of people.*
Die belauschen sie mit Lust,	*They listen to you with pleasure—*
Rufen, wenn der Tag erwacht:	*cry out, when the day breaks:*
Kehre wieder, heil'ge Nacht,	*Come back, hallowed night;*
Holde Träume, kehret wieder.	*lovely dreams, come back.*

Nachtstück

poem by Johann Baptist Mayrhofer

D 672. Original key: C minor. Composed in October, 1819, Schubert's first draft was in C-sharp minor, and differs slightly from the published version. Possibly the copy made for the printer and representing Schubert's last thoughts was in C minor, because the *Neue Ausgabe* prints versions in both keys. The song is dedicated to the opera singer Katharina von Lászny, and was published by Cappi in February, 1825, as Opus 36, No. 2. See "Abendstern" for notes on Mayrhofer.

Nachtstück	*Nocturne*
Wenn über Berge sich der Nebel breitet,	*When, over mountains, the mist spreads itself,*
Und Luna mit Gewölken kämpft,	*and the moon battles with the clouds,*
So nimmt der Alte seine Harfe und schreitet	*then the old man takes his harp and sets about*
Und singt waldeinwärts und gedämpft:	*and sings into the woods, and quietly:*
Du heil'ge Nacht,	*"You holy night,*
Bald ist's vollbracht,	*soon will it be done;*
Bald schlaf ich ihn,	*soon shall I sleep*
Den langen Schlummer,	*the long slumber*
Der mich erlöst	*which will deliver me*
Von allem Kummer.	*from all trouble."*
Die grünen Bäume rauschen dann:	*The green trees rustle then:*
Schlaf süß, du guter alter Mann;	*"Sleep sweetly, you good old man."*
Die Gräser lispeln wankend fort:	*The grasses whisper, wavering forward:*
Wir decken seinen Ruheort;	*"We shall cover his resting place."*
Und mancher liebe Vogel ruft:	*And many a dear bird calls:*
O lasst ihn ruhn in Rasengruft.	*"Oh let him rest in the grass-covered grave!"*
Der Alte horcht, der Alte schweigt,	*The old man listens, the old man is silent;*
Der Tod hat sich zu ihm geneigt.	*death has bent down to him.*

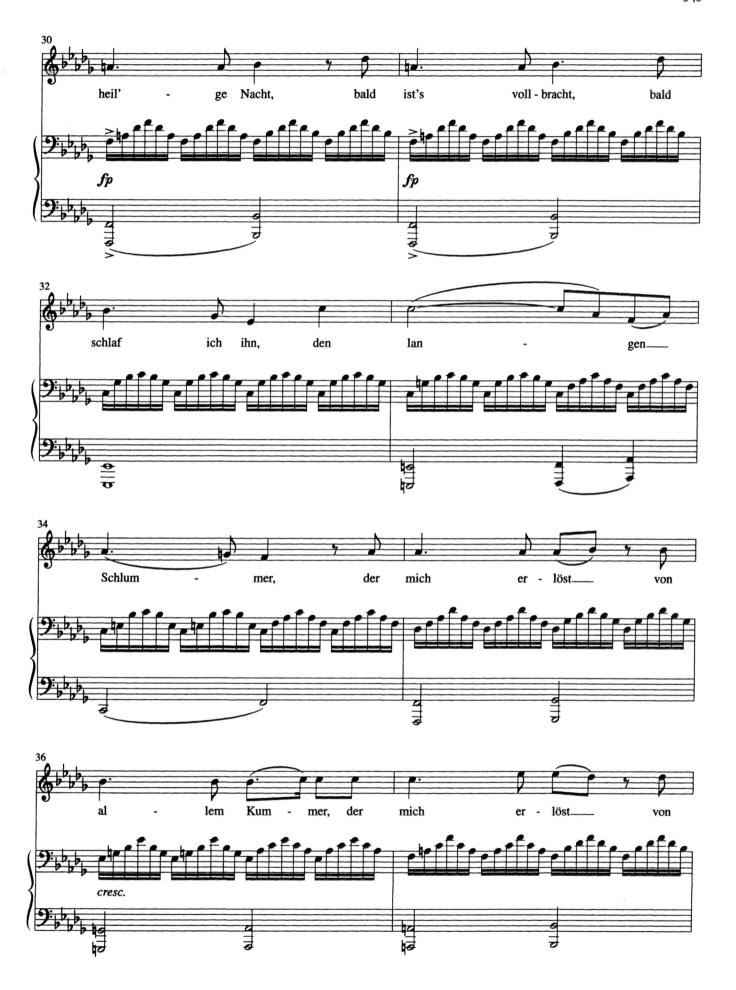

wan - kend fort:____ Wir de - cken sei - nen Ru - he - ort; die

grü - nen Bäu - me rau - schen dann: Schlaf süß, du gu - ter____

al - ter Mann; und man - cher lie - be Vo - gel ruft:____ O

lasst ihn ruhn____ in____ Ra - sen-gruft, o lasst ihn ruhn____ in____

Nachtviolen

poem by Johann Baptist Mayrhofer

D 752. Original key: C major. This song, according to a copy in the Witteczek-Spaun collection, was composed in April, 1822, a few months after Schubert had moved out of the home he shared with Mayrhofer. The first published version, by J.P. Gotthard, in 1872, was in A-flat, and although a note on the Witteczek-Spaun copy suggests A-flat was the original key, no manuscript copy in that key exists. Mayrhofer's title, when published in 1824, was "Nachtviolenlied" [Nightviolets' Song], and it may have originally been part of his "Heliopolis" cycle. See "Abendstern" for notes on Mayrhofer. Also see "Heliopolis I."

Nachtviolen	*Nightviolets*
Nachtviolen, Nachtviolen,	*Nightviolets, nightviolets,*
Dunkle Augen, seelenvolle,	*dark eyes, soulful,*
Selig ist es, sich versenken	*blissful it is to sink*
In dem samtnen Blau.	*in the velvet blue.*
Grüne Blätter streben freudig	*Green leaves strive cheerfully*
Euch zu hellen, euch zu schmücken,	*to brighten you, to adorn you;*
Doch ihr blicket ernst und schweigend	*but you look solemnly and silently*
In die laue Frühlingsluft.	*into the mild spring air.*
Mit erhabnem Wehmutsstrahle	*With a sublime ray of melancholy*
Trafet ihr mein treues Herz,	*you touched my faithful heart;*
Und nun blüht in stummen Nächten	*and now, in speechless nights, blooms*
Fort die heilige Verbindung.	*forth the sacred union.*

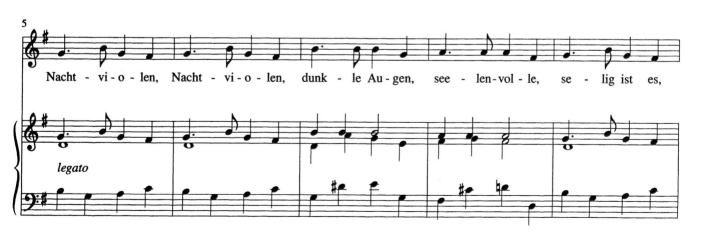

sich ver - sen - ken in dem samt - nen Blau, in dem samt - nen Blau.

Grü - ne Blät - ter stre - ben freu - dig euch zu hel - len, euch zu schmü - cken,

doch ihr bli - cket ernst und schwei - gend in die lau - e Früh - lings - luft.

Mit er - hab - nem Weh - muts - strah - le

Romanze

poem by Wilhelmine Christiane von Chézy

D 797. Original key. First performed by Emilie Neumann in December, 1823, the same month it was composed, this aria is from the incidental music for *Rosamunde*, and was published with piano accompaniment in March, 1824. Chézy (1783–1856) is best known for her libretto for Weber's *Euryanthe* and as the poet for the middle section of Schubert's "Der Hirt auf dem Felsen," for voice, piano and clarinet obbligato.

Romanze

Der Vollmond strahlt auf Bergeshöhn,
Wie hab ich dich vermisst!
Du süßes Herz, es ist so schön,
Wenn treu die Treue küsst.

Was frommt des Maien holde Zier?
Du warst mein Frühlingsstrahl.
Licht meiner Nacht, o lächle mir
Im Tode noch einmal.

Sie trat hinein beim Vollmondschein,
Sie blickte himmelwärts:
»Im Leben fern, im Tode dein!«
Und sanft brach Herz an Herz.

Romance

The full moon shines upon mountaintops;
how I have missed you!
You sweet heart, it is so beautiful
when truly the true one kisses.

To what avail is May's lovely finery?
You were my ray of spring.
Light of my night, oh smile upon me,
in death, once more.

She went out into the light of the full moon;
she looked heavenwards:
"In life distant, in death yours!"
And softly broke heart on heart.

Schäfers Klagelied

poem by Johann Wolfgang von Goethe

D 121. Original key. Composed on November 30, 1814, this was the first Schubert song to be performed in public. Franz Jager, a tenor from the Karnenthor Theater in Vienna, premiered it on February 28, 1819, transposed to the key of E minor; Schubert also added a short introduction. Both versions are included in the *Neue Ausgabe*. It was published with a dedication to Ignaz von Mosel, in May, 1821, by Cappi and Diabelli, and designated Opus 3, No. 1. See "An den Mond" for notes on Goethe.

Schäfers Klagelied	Shepherd's Lament
Da droben auf jenem Berge	*Up there on that hill,*
Da steh ich tausendmal,	*there stand I thousands of times*
An meinem Stabe hingebogen	*leaning on my staff,*
Und schaue hinab in das Tal.	*and I gaze down into the valley.*
Dann folg ich der weidenden Herde,	*Then I follow the grazing herd;*
Mein Hündchen bewahret mir sie.	*my dear dog protects them for me.*
Ich bin herunter gekommen	*I have come down here*
Und weiß doch selber nicht wie.	*and yet know not, myself, why.*
Da stehet von schönen Blumen,	*There stands the whole meadow*
Die ganze Wiese so voll,	*so full of beautiful flowers;*
Ich breche sie, ohne zu wissen,	*I pick them without knowing*
Wem ich sie geben soll.	*to whom I should give them.*
Und Regen, Sturm und Gewitter	*And rain, storm and tempest*
Verpass' ich unter dem Baum.	*I weather beneath the tree.*
Die Türe dort bleibet verschlossen;	*The door over there remains locked;*
Doch alles ist leider ein Traum.	*for all is, sadly, a dream.*
Es stehet ein Regenbogen	*There is a rainbow*
Wohl über jenem Haus!	*right above that house!*
Sie aber ist fortgezogen,	*She, however, has gone away,*
Und weit in das Land hinaus.	*and far, to distant lands.*
Hinaus in das Land und weiter,	*To distant lands and beyond,*
Vielleicht gar über die See.	*perhaps even over the sea.*
Vorüber, ihr Schafe! nur vorüber,	*Go on, you sheep, just go on!*
Dem Schäfer ist gar so weh.	*The shepherd is so very sad.*

Sta - be hin - ge - bo - gen und schau - e hin - ab in das Tal.

pp   pp

Dann folg ich der wei - den - den Her - de, mein Hünd - chen be - wah - ret mir sie. Ich

p

bin— her - un - ter ge - kom - men und weiß doch sel - ber nicht wie.

cresc.   p

Da ste - het von schö - nen Blu - men, da steht— die gan - ze

pp

24

Wie - se so voll, ich bre - che sie, oh - ne zu wis - sen, wem ich sie ge - ben

zurückhaltend

28

soll. Und Re - gen, Sturm und Ge - wit - ter ver-

f

31

pass' ich un - ter dem Baum. Die

ff *fz* *fz*

34

Tü - re dort blei - bet ver - schlos - sen; doch al - les ist lei - der ein Traum.

pp

Rastlose Liebe

poem by Johann Wolfgang von Goethe

D 138. Original key: E major. Composed on May 19, 1815, this song was dedicated to Anton Salieri and published in July of 1821, as Opus 5, No. 1, by Cappi and Diabelli. Goethe penned his poem in May of 1771, during a stay in the Thuringian Forest, two days after a snowstorm. There are two autographs, and the second, in D major, is also included in the *Neue Ausgabe*. This was one of Schubert's earliest successes, and an excerpt from his diary dated June 14, 1816 describes a performance at the home of Count Erdody on June 13: "I too had to perform on this occasion... I played variations by Beethoven, sang Goethe's 'Rastlose Liebe' and Schiller's 'Amalia.' The first [lied] was enthusiastically received, the second less so... one cannot deny that Goethe's musical and poetic genius was largely responsible for the applause." Schubert repeats the last line of the poem, altering it to, "O Liebe, bist du!" [oh love, are you!]. See "An den Mond" for notes on Goethe.

Rastlose Liebe	Restless Love
Dem Schnee, dem Regen,	*Against the snow, the rain,*
Dem Wind entgegen,	*the wind,*
Im Dampf der Klüfte,	*in the mist of the ravines,*
Durch Nebeldüfte,	*through foggy vapors,*
Immer zu, immer zu,	*ever onward, ever onward,*
Ohne Rast und Ruh!	*without repose or rest!*
Lieber durch Leiden	*Rather through suffering*
Möcht' ich mich schlagen,	*would I fight my way,*
Als so viel Freuden	*than to bear*
Des Lebens ertragen!	*so much of life's joy!*
Alle das Neigen	*All the inclining*
Von Herzen zu Herzen,	*of heart to heart—*
Ach, wie so eigen	*ah, how it in its own way*
Schaffet das Schmerzen!	*creates pain!*
Wie soll ich fliehn?	*How shall I flee?*
Wälderwärts ziehn!	*Go toward the forest?*
Alles vergebens!	*All in vain!*
Krone des Lebens,	*Crown of life,*
Glück ohne Ruh,	*happiness without rest,*
Liebe, bist du!	*love, are you!*

Liebesbotschaft

poem by Ludwig Rellstab

D 957, No. 1. Original key: G major. This is one of seven Rellstab poems which form part of *Schwanengesang*. Schubert set many poems on the subject of water, and more specifically streams and brooks (e.g. "Die Forelle," "Wohin"). This is his final "brook" song. *Schwanengesang* [Swan Song], fourteen songs set to the poetry of Rellstab, Heine, and Seidl, was published in May of 1829, by Tobias Haslinger. The title, Haslinger's own, was meant to advertise these songs of Schubert as "the last blossoming of his noble art." There is evidence that Schubert would have published the Rellstab and Heine songs, composed in 1827–1828, as separate groupings, if he could have found a publisher to accept them. One month after Schubert's passing, his brother, Ferdinand, sold the Rellstab and Heine songs to Haslinger, perhaps to fulfill an agreement previously made by Schubert himself. Haslinger published the songs in two volumes. Volume I included the first six Rellstab songs, and Volume II the seventh Rellstab song, six Heine songs and Seidl's "Die Taubenpost." Haslinger included the Seidl setting because it, too, represented one of Schubert's "last blossomings." Rellstab (1799–1860), a fine pianist in his youth, became a noted poet, novelist and one of the first professional music critics. In addition to his connection with Schubert, he was acquainted with Beethoven, who considered collaborating with him on an opera.

Liebesbotschaft	*Love's Message*
Rauschendes Bächlein,	*Murmuring brooklet,*
So silbern und hell,	*so silvery and bright,*
Eilst zur Geliebten	*are you hurrying to my beloved,*
So munter und schnell?	*so merrily and swiftly?*
Ach, trautes Bächlein,	*Ah, dear brooklet,*
Mein Bote sei du;	*my messenger may you be;*
Bringe die Grüße	*bring the greetings*
Des Fernen ihr zu.	*of the distant one to her.*
All ihre Blumen,	*All her flowers,*
Im Garten gepflegt,	*in her garden tended,*
Die sie so lieblich	*which she so charmingly*
Am Busen trägt,	*on her bosom wears,*
Und ihre Rosen	*and her roses*
In purpurner Glut,	*in crimson glow,*
Bächlein, erquicke	*brooklet, refresh*
Mit kühlender Flut.	*with cooling waters.*
Wann sie am Ufer,	*When she, on the bank,*
In Träume versenkt,	*lost in dreams,*
Meiner gedenkend	*thinking of me*
Das Köpfchen hängt,	*inclines her head,*
Tröste die Süße	*comfort the sweet one*
Mit freundlichem Blick,	*with a friendly glance,*
Denn der Geliebte	*for her beloved*
Kehrt bald zurück.	*will soon return.*
Neigt sich die Sonne	*When the sun wanes*
Mit rötlichem Schein,	*with reddish sheen,*
Wiege das Liebchen	*rock the darling*
In Schlummer ein,	*to sleep,*
Rausche sie murmelnd	*murmur her*
In süße Ruh,	*into sweet peace;*
Flüstre ihr Träume	*whisper to her dreams*
Der Liebe zu.	*of love.*

Rau - schen-des Bäch - lein, so sil - bern und hell,

eilst zur Ge-lieb - ten so mun - ter und schnell?

rück.

decresc.

Neigt sich die Son - ne mit röt - li-chem Schein,

pp

wie - ge das Lieb - chen in Schlum - mer ein,

rau - sche sie mur - melnd in sü - ße— Ruh,

flüst - re ihr Träu - me der Lie - be zu,

flüst - re ihr Träu - me der

Lie - be zu.

pp

dim.

Kriegers Ahnung

poem by Ludwig Rellstab

D 957, No. 2. Original key. This is one of seven Rellstab poems which form part of *Schwanengesang*. See "Liebesbotschaft" for notes on Rellstab and *Schwanengesang*.

Kriegers Ahnung	*Soldier's Presentiment*
In tiefer Ruh liegt um mich her	*In deep repose lie around me*
Der Waffenbrüder Kreis.	*the circle of fellow soldiers.*
Mir ist das Herz so bang und schwer,	*My heart is so anxious and heavy,*
Von Sehnsucht mir so heiß.	*so ardent with longing.*
Wie hab ich oft so süß geträumt	*How often have I so sweetly dreamed*
An ihrem Busen warm,	*upon her warm bosom;*
Wie freundlich schien des Herdes Glut,	*how cheerful seemed the hearth's glow*
Lag sie in meinem Arm.	*as she lay in my arms.*
Hier, wo der Flammen düstrer Schein,	*Here, where the gleam of melancholy flames*
Ach, nur auf Waffen spielt,	*alas, only upon weapons plays,*
Hier fühlt die Brust sich ganz allein,	*here the heart feels utterly alone;*
Der Wehmut Träne quillt.	*a tear of sadness wells up.*
Herz, dass der Trost dich nicht verlässt,	*Heart, may comfort not desert you;*
Es ruft noch manche Schlacht.	*many a battle still calls.*
Bald ruh ich wohl und schlafe fest,	*Soon shall I rest well and sleep soundly.*
Herzliebste—gute Nacht.	*Dearest beloved, goodnight.*

quillt, der Weh - mut Trä - ne quillt.

Geschwind, unruhig

Herz, dass der Trost dich nicht ver - lässt, dass der

Trost dich nicht ver - lässt, es ruft noch man - che

Frühlingssehnsucht

poem by Ludwig Rellstab

D 957, No. 3. Original key: B-flat major. This is one of seven Rellstab poems which form part of *Schwanengesang*. See "Liebesbotschaft" for notes on Rellstab and *Schwanengesang*.

Frühlingssehnsucht	Spring Longing
Säuselnde Lüfte	*Whispering breezes*
Wehend so mild,	*blowing so mild,*
Blumiger Düfte	*with flower fragrances*
Atmend erfüllt!	*breathing, filled!*
Wie haucht ihr mich wonnig begrüßend an!	*How rapturously welcomed you breathe upon me!*
Wie habt ihr dem pochenden Herzen getan?	*What have you done to my throbbing heart?*
Es möchte euch folgen auf luftiger Bahn!	*It wants to follow you on your airy path!*
Wohin?	*Whither?*
Bächlein so munter,	*Brooklets so merrily*
Rauschend zumal,	*rushing especially*
Wollen hinunter	*want to go down,*
Silbern ins Tal.	*silvery, into the valley.*
Die schwebende Welle, dort eilt sie dahin!	*The gliding ripples hurry thither!*
Tief spiegeln sich Fluren und Himmel darin.	*Deeply mirrored therein are meadows and heavens.*
Was ziehst du mich, sehnend verlangender Sinn,	*Why do you draw me, longingly desiring senses,*
Hinab?	*down there?*
Grüßender Sonne	*From the welcoming sun's*
Spielendes Gold,	*glittering gold,*
Hoffende Wonne	*hopeful joy*
Bringest du hold.	*bring you graciously.*
Wie labt mich dein selig begrüßendes Bild!	*How your happy, welcoming image refreshes me!*
Es lächelt am tiefblauen Himmel so mild	*It smiles in the deep blue heaven so tenderly*
Und hat mir das Auge mit Tränen gefüllt.	*and has filled my eyes with tears.*
Warum?	*Why?*
Grünend umkränzet	*Greening bedecks*
Wälder und Höh,	*woods and summits;*
Schimmernd erglänzet	*shimmering sparkles*
Blütenschnee.	*the snow blossom.*
So dränget sich alles zum bräutlichen Licht,	*So does everything press toward the bridal light:*
Es schwellen die Keime, die Knospe bricht,	*the seeds swell, the bud bursts;*
Sie haben gefunden, was ihnen gebricht,	*they have found what they needed—*
Und du?	*and you?*
Rastloses Sehnen,	*Restless longing,*
Wünschendes Herz,	*yearning heart,*
Immer nur Tränen,	*always only tears,*
Klage und Schmerz?	*lament and pain?*
Auch ich bin mir schwellender Triebe bewusst,	*I too am conscious of swelling urges.*
Wer stillet mir endlich die drängende Lust?	*Who will at last quiet my pressing desire?*
Nur du befreist den Lenz in der Brust,	*Only you will set free the spring in my breast,*
Nur du!	*only you!*

Düf - te at - mend er - füllt!_____ Wie
un - ter sil - bern ins Tal._____ Die

haucht ihr mich won - nig be - grü - ßend an! Wie
schwe - ben - de Wel - le, dort eilt sie da - hin! Tief

habt ihr dem po - chen - den Her - zen ge - tan? Es
spie - geln sich Flu - ren und Him - mel da - rin. Was

möch - te euch fol - gen auf luf - ti - ger Bahn, es
ziehst du mich, seh - nend ver - lan - gen - der Sinn, was

Ständchen

poem by Ludwig Rellstab

D 957, No. 4. Original key: D minor. This is one of seven Rellstab poems which form part of *Schwanengesang*.
See "Liebesbotschaft" for notes on Rellstab and *Schwanengesang*.

Ständchen	Serenade
Leise flehen meine Lieder	*Gently plead my songs*
Durch die Nacht zu dir,	*through the night to you;*
In den stillen Hain hernieder,	*into the quiet grove below,*
Liebchen, komm zu mir.	*sweetheart, come to me.*
Flüsternd schlanke Wipfel rauschen	*Whispering, slender treetops rustle*
In des Mondes Licht,	*in the moon's light;*
Des Verräters feindlich Lauschen	*of a betrayer's unfriendly eavesdropping*
Fürchte, Holde, nicht.	*be not afraid, lovely one.*
Hörst die Nachtigallen schlagen?	*Do you hear the nightingales' call?*
Ach! sie flehen dich,	*Ah, they implore you;*
Mit der Töne süßen Klagen	*with the sound of sweet laments*
Flehen sie für mich.	*they plead to you for me.*
Sie verstehn des Busens Sehnen,	*They understand the heart's longing;*
Kennen Liebesschmerz,	*they know love's pain.*
Rühren mit den Silbertönen	*They stir, with silvery tones,*
Jedes weiche Herz.	*every tender heart.*
Lass auch dir die Brust bewegen,	*Let your heart also be moved;*
Liebchen, höre mich!	*sweetheart, hear me!*
Bebend harr ich dir entgegen,	*Trembling, I await you;*
Komm, beglücke mich.	*come, make me happy.*

fürch - te, Hol - de, nicht,   fürch - te, Hol - de, nicht.
je - des wei - che Herz,   je - des wei - che

Herz.   Lass auch dir die Brust be - we - gen,   Lieb - chen, hö - re

mich!　Be - bend harr ich dir ent-ge - gen,

komm, be-glü - cke mich,　komm, be-glü - cke

mich,＿＿＿＿＿＿　be - glü - cke　mich.

decresc.

dim.

Aufenthalt

poem by Ludwig Rellstab

D 957, No. 5. Original key: E minor. This is one of seven Rellstab poems which form part of *Schwanengesang*. See "Liebesbotschaft" for notes on Rellstab and *Schwanengesang*.

Aufenthalt	*Resting Place*
Rauschender Strom,	*Roaring river,*
Brausender Wald,	*blustering forest,*
Starrender Fels	*towering cliff:*
Mein Aufenthalt.	*my resting place.*
Wie sich die Welle	*As wave*
An Welle reiht,	*follows upon wave,*
Fließen die Tränen	*so flow my tears*
Mir ewig erneut.	*ever anew.*
Hoch in den Kronen	*The high treetops*
Wogend sich's regt,	*stir with undulation;*
So unaufhörlich	*so unceasingly*
Mein Herze schlägt.	*my heart beats.*
Und wie des Felsen	*And like the rock's*
Uraltes Erz	*ageless ore,*
Ewig derselbe	*forever the same*
Bleibet mein Schmerz.	*remains my sorrow.*

This page is blank to facilitate page turns.

In der Ferne

poem by Ludwig Rellstab

D 957, No. 6. Original key: B minor. This is one of seven Rellstab poems which form part of *Schwanengesang*.
See "Liebesbotschaft" for notes on Rellstab and *Schwanengesang*.

In der Ferne	Far Away
Wehe dem Fliehenden,	*Woe to those who flee,*
Welt hinaus Ziehenden!—	*those who go out into the world!—*
Fremde Durchmessenden,	*those who travel through foreign places,*
Heimat Vergessenden,	*those who forget their homeland,*
Mutterhaus Hassenden,	*those who spurn their mother's home,*
Freunde Verlassenden	*those who forsake friends:*
Folget kein Segen, ach,	*no blessing follows, alas,*
Auf ihren Wegen nach!	*upon their paths!*
Herze! das sehnende,	*Heart, yearning,*
Auge, das tränende,	*eye, weeping,*
Sehnsucht, nie endende,	*longing, never-ending,*
Heimwärts sich wendende,	*homeward turning;*
Busen, der wallende,	*bosom surging,*
Klage, verhallende,	*lament fading,*
Abendstern, blinkender,	*evening star, twinkling,*
Hoffnungslos sinkender.	*without hopes sinking.*
Lüfte, ihr säuselnden,	*Breezes, you whispering ones,*
Wellen sanft kräuselnden,	*waves softly ruffled,*
Sonnenstrahl, eilender,	*sunbeams speeding,*
Nirgend verweilender:	*nowhere lingering:*
Die mir mit Schmerze, ach!	*take to her who with pain, alas,*
Dies treue Herze brach,	*broke this faithful heart,*
Grüßt von dem Fliehenden,	*greetings from the fleeing one,*
Welt hinaus Ziehenden.	*the one gone out into the world.*

Sehn - sucht, nie en - den - de, heim - wärts sich wen - den - de, Bu - sen, der

wal - len - de, Kla - ge, ver - hal - len - de, A - bend - stern, blin - ken - der,

hoff - nungs - los sin - ken - der, hoff - nungs - los sin - ken - der.

Lüf - te, ihr säu - seln - den, Wel - len sanft

Abschied

poem by Ludwig Rellstab

D 957, No. 7. Original key: E-flat major. This is one of seven Rellstab poems which form part of *Schwanengesang*. See "Liebesbotschaft" for notes on Rellstab and *Schwanengesang*.

Abschied

Ade! du muntre, du fröhliche Stadt, ade!
Schon scharret mein Rösslein mit lustigem Fuß,
Jetzt nimm meinen letzten, den scheidenden Gruß,
Du hast mich wohl niemals noch traurig gesehn,
So kann es auch jetzt nicht beim Abschied geschehn,
Ade! du muntre, du fröhliche Stadt, ade!

Ade! ihr Bäume, ihr Gärten so grün, ade!
Nun reit ich am silbernen Strome entlang,
Weit schallend ertönet mein Abschiedsgesang,
Nie habt ihr ein trauriges Lied gehört,
So wird euch auch keines beim Scheiden beschert,
Ade! ihr Bäume, ihr Gärten so grün, ade!

Ade! ihr freundlichen Mägdlein dort, ade!
Was schaut ihr aus blumenumduftetem Haus
Mit schelmischen, lockenden Blicken heraus!
Wie sonst, so grüß ich und schaue mich um,
Doch nimmer wend ich mein Rösslein um,
Ade! ihr freundlichen Mägdlein dort, ade!

Ade! liebe Sonne, so gehst du zur Ruh! Ade!
Nun schimmert der blinkenden Sterne Gold,
Wie bin ich euch Sternlein am Himmel so hold,
Durchziehn wir die Welt auch weit und breit,
Ihr gebt überall uns das treue Geleit,
Ade! liebe Sonne, so gehst du zur Ruh, ade!

Ade! du schimmerndes Fensterlein hell, ade!
Du glänzest so traulich mit dämmerndem Schein
Und ladest so freundlich ins Hüttchen uns ein.
Vorüber, ach, ritt ich so manches mal,
Und wär es denn heute zum letzten mal,
Ade! du schimmerndes Fensterlein hell, ade!

Ade! ihr Sterne, verhüllet euch grau! Ade!
Des Fensterlein trübes, verschimmerndes Licht
Ersetzt ihr unzähligen Sterne mir nicht;
Darf ich hier nicht weilen, muss hier vorbei,
Was hilft es, folgt ihr mir noch so treu,
Ade! ihr Sterne, verhüllet euch grau, ade!

Parting

Farewell, you lively, happy town, farewell!
Already my horse is pawing with joyful hoof.
Now accept my last, parting greeting.
You have never yet seen me sad;
so neither can it happen now at parting.
Farewell, you lively, happy town, farewell!

Farewell, you trees, you gardens so green, farewell!
Now I shall ride alongside the silvery river;
far echoing will resound my parting song.
Never have you heard a sad song;
so neither will one be given you at parting.
Farewell, you trees, you gardens so green, farewell!

Farewell, you friendly maidens there, farewell!
Why do you gaze from flower-fragrant houses
with teasing, enticing looks?
As always, so will I greet you and look back;
but never will I turn my horse back.
Farewell, you friendly maidens there, farewell!

Farewell, dear sun, as you go to rest! Farewell!
Now shimmers the gold of twinkling stars.
How fond I am of you little stars in the sky;
as we traverse the world both far and wide
you provide for us everywhere the faithful escort.
Farewell, dear sun, as you go to rest, farewell!

Farewell, you little window glimmering bright, farewell!
You shine so cosily with twilight glow
and invite us so amiably into the little cottage.
Past by, ah, I rode so many a time;
and might it then be today for the last time?
Farewell, you little window glimmering bright, farewell!

Farewell, you stars; veil yourselves in grey! Farewell!
The little window's faint, fading light
you innumerable stars can not replace for me.
If I can not tarry here, if I must pass by,
what help is it, though you follow me ever so faithfully!
Farewell, you stars; veil yourselves in grey, farewell!

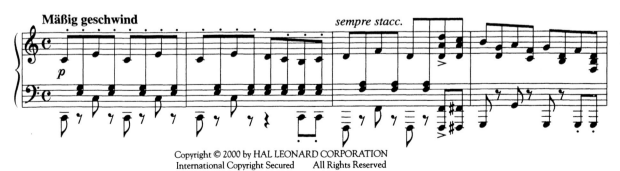

Ab - schied ge-schehn, so kann es auch jetzt nicht beim Ab - schied ge-schehn, a - de! du

munt - re, du fröh - li - che Stadt, a - de!

A - de! ihr

Bäu - me, ihr Gär - ten so grün, a - de! Nun

Röss - lein um, a - de! ihr freund - li - chen Mägd - lein dort, a -

de!

A - de! lie - be Son - ne, so gehst du zur Ruh! A -

de! Nun schim - mert der blin - ken - den Ster - ne Gold, wie

de! du schim - mern - des Fens - ter - lein hell, a - de!

Du glän - zest so trau - lich mit däm - mern - dem Schein und la - dest so freund - lich ins

Hütt - chen uns ein. Vor - ü - ber, ach, ritt ich so man - ches mal, und wär es denn heu - te zum

letz - ten mal, und wär es denn heu - te zum letz - ten mal, a - de! du

hier____ nicht wei - len, muss hier____ vor-bei, was hilft es, folgt ihr mir noch so treu, darf ich

hier nicht wei - len, muss hier vor-bei, was hilft es, folgt ihr mir noch so treu, a -

de! ihr Ster - ne, ver-hül - let euch grau, a - de!____

Der Atlas

poem by Heinrich Heine

D 957, No. 8. Original key: G minor. Atlas led the Titans in war against Zeus. Once they were defeated, Atlas was forced to carry the sky on his shoulders as punishment. Heine (1797–1856) was the son of a Düsseldorf merchant. After a short and disastrous career in business, he turned to law, studying in Bonn and Göttingen. In later life he lived in Paris, writing in French as well as in German. Heine was the poet for six of the songs which comprise *Schwanengesang*, but his fame as a poet rests more on the poems set by Robert Schumann than on those in *Schwanengesang*. The *Schwanengesang* poems, the only Heine verses set by Schubert, come from a cycle called *Die Heimkehr* [The Homecoming], written in 1823–1824. As with the Rellstab poems included in *Schwanengesang*, Schubert's intent was to publish the Heine songs separately. In that case he would probably have had the songs published in Heine's order (3,5,4,6,2,1), since it was his practice to respect the intention of the poet in such matters. Heine left the *Schwanengesang* poems untitled; the titles are Schubert's. See "Liebesbotschaft" for notes on *Schwanengesang*.

Der Atlas	Atlas
Ich unglücksel'ger Atlas, eine Welt,	I, unhappy Atlas! A world—
Die ganze Welt der Schmerzen muss ich tragen,	the whole world of affliction—must I bear.
Ich trage Unerträgliches, und brechen	I bear the unbearable, though break
Will mir das Herz im Leibe.	would my heart within my body.
Du stolzes Herz, du hast es ja gewollt,	You proud heart, you have so willed it.
Du wolltest glücklich sein, unendlich glücklich,	You wanted to be happy, endlessly happy,
Oder unendlich elend, stolzes Herz,	or endlessly miserable, proud heart;
Und jetzo bist du elend.	and now you are miserable.

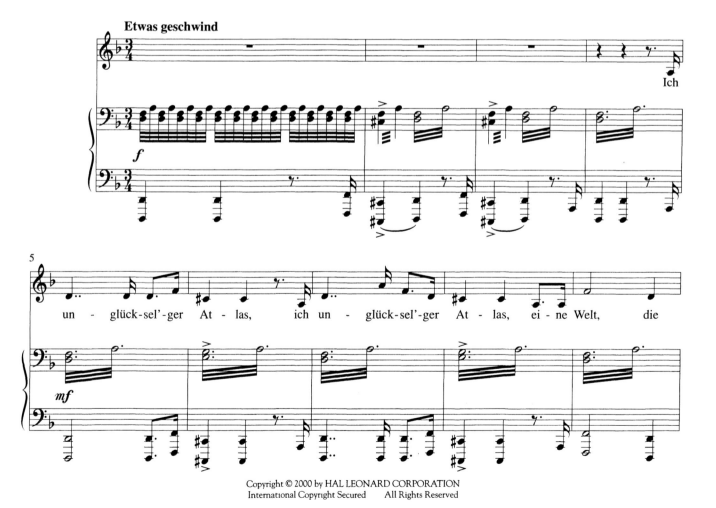

Ihr Bild

poem by Heinrich Heine

D 957, No. 9. Original key: B-flat minor. This is one of six Heine poems which form part of *Schwanengesang*. See "Der Atlas" for notes on Heine. See "Liebesbotschaft" for notes on *Schwanengesang*.

Ihr Bild	Her Picture
Ich stand in dunkeln Träumen	*I stood in dark dreams*
Und starrt' ihr Bildnis an,	*and stared at her portrait,*
Und das geliebte Antlitz	*and the beloved face*
Heimlich zu leben begann.	*mysteriously began to come to life.*
Um ihre Lippen zog sich	*Around her lips stretched*
Ein Lächeln, wunderbar,	*a smile, wondrous;*
Und wie von Wehmutstränen	*and as though with tears of sadness*
Erglänzte ihr Augenpaar.	*her eyes glistened.*
Auch meine Tränen flossen	*My tears, too, flowed*
Mir von den Wangen herab—	*down my cheeks—*
Und ach, ich kann es nicht glauben,	*and ah, I can not believe it,*
dass ich dich verloren hab.	*that I have lost you.*

Lä - cheln, wun - der - bar, und wie von Weh - muts - trä - nen er - glänz - te ihr Au - gen -

cresc.

paar. Auch mei - ne Trä - nen flos - sen mir

pp

von den Wan - gen her - ab— und ach, ich kann es nicht

cresc.

glau - ben, dass ich dich ver - lo - ren hab.

f

Das Fischermädchen

poem by Heinrich Heine

D 957, No. 10. Original key: A-flat major. This is one of six Heine poems which form part of *Schwanengesang*. See "Der Atlas" for notes on Heine. See "Liebesbotschaft" for notes on *Schwanengesang*.

Das Fischermädchen

Du schönes Fischermädchen,
Treibe den Kahn ans Land—
Komm zu mir und setze dich nieder,
Wir kosen Hand in Hand.

Leg an mein Herz dein Köpfchen
Und fürchte dich nicht zu sehr,
Vertraust du dich doch sorglos
Täglich dem wilden Meer.

Mein Herz gleicht ganz dem Meere,
Hat Sturm und Ebb' und Flut,
Und manche schöne Perle
In seiner Tiefe ruht.

The Fishermaiden

You lovely fishermaiden,
guide the boat to the shore—
Come to me and sit down;
we will talk of love, hand in hand.

Lay upon my heart your little head,
and be not afraid too much;
for you entrust yourself fearlessly
every day to the turbulent sea.

My heart is just like the sea:
it has storms and ebbs and floods;
and many a beautiful pearl
rests in its depths.

35
traust du dich_ doch sorg-los täg-lich dem wil-den Meer, ver-

39
traust du dich_ doch sorg - los täg-lich dem wil - den Meer,____

43
täg-lich dem wil - den Meer.

47
Mein Herz gleicht ganz_ dem Mee - re, hat

Die Stadt

poem by Heinrich Heine

D 957, No. 11. Original key: C minor. This is one of six Heine poems which form part of *Schwanengesang*. The city with its towers may be Hamburg (Hamburg's coat of arms shows three towers). It was here that Heine met, loved, and lost Amalie, his beautiful cousin. See "Der Atlas" for notes on Heine. See "Liebesbotschaft" for notes on *Schwanengesang*.

Die Stadt	The City
Am fernen Horizonte	On the distant horizon
Erscheint, wie ein Nebelbild,	appears, as a misty image,
Die Stadt mit ihren Türmen,	the city with its towers,
In Abenddämmrung gehüllt.	veiled in evening's dusk.
Ein feuchter Windzug kräuselt	A dank gust of wind ruffles
Die graue Wasserbahn;	the grey waterway;
Mit traurigem Takte rudert	with melancholy strokes
Der Schiffer in meinem Kahn.	the boatman rows my boat.
Die Sonne hebt sich noch einmal	The sun rises once again,
Leuchtend vom Boden empor	shining from the bottom of the sea upwards,
Und zeigt mir jene Stelle,	and shows me that place
Wo ich das Liebste verlor.	where I lost my dearest love.

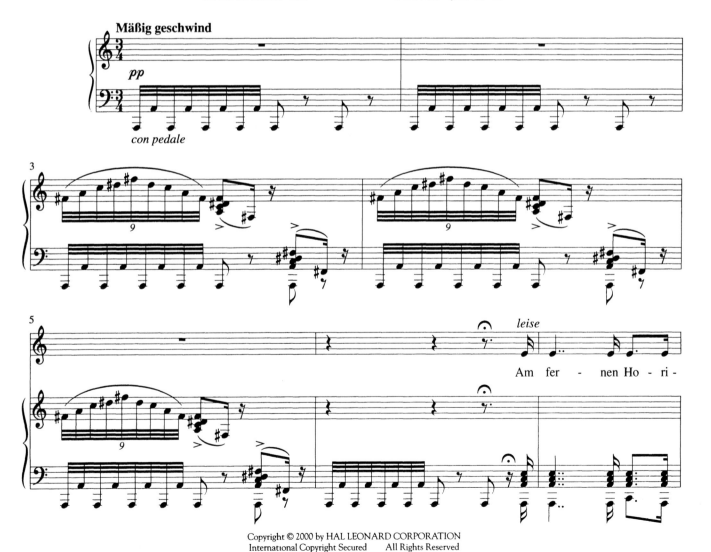

zon - te er-scheint, wie ein Ne - bel - bild, die Stadt mit ih - ren

Tür - men, in A - bend-dämm - rung ge - hüllt.

Ein feuch - ter Wind - zug

Die Son - ne hebt sich noch ein - mal leuch-tend vom Bo - den em-

por und zeigt mir je - ne Stel - le, wo ich das Liebs - te ver-

lor.

Die Son - ne hebt sich noch ein - mal leuch-tend vom Bo - den em-

por und zeigt mir je - ne Stel - le, wo ich das Liebs - te ver-

lor.

Am Meer

poem by Heinrich Heine

D 957, No. 12. Original key: C major. This is one of six Heine poems which form part of *Schwanengesang*. It is also Schubert's last strophic song. See "Der Atlas" for notes on Heine. See "Liebesbotschaft" for notes on *Schwanengesang*.

Am Meer

Das Meer erglänzte weit hinaus
Im letzten Abendscheine,
Wir saßen am einsamen Fischerhaus,
Wir saßen stumm und alleine.

Der Nebel stieg, das Wasser schwoll,
Die Möwe flog hin und wieder;
Aus deinen Augen, liebevoll,
Fielen die Tränen nieder.

Ich sah sie fallen auf deine Hand
Und bin auf's Knie gesunken,
Ich hab von deiner weißen Hand
Die Tränen fortgetrunken.

Seit jener Stunde verzehrt sich mein Leib,
Die Seele stirbt vor Sehnen;—
Mich hat das unglücksel'ge Weib
vergiftet mit ihren Tränen.

By the Sea

The sea glistened far into the distance
in the last light of evening.
We sat by the fisherman's solitary house;
we sat silent and alone.

The mist lifted, the water swelled,
the seagull flew to and fro;
from your eyes, full of love,
fell the tears down.

I saw them fall upon your hand,
and sank to my knees;
from your white hand
I drank away the tears.

Since that hour my body wastes away,
my soul dies of longing;—
the miserable woman has
poisoned me with her tears.

Der Doppelgänger

poem by Heinrich Heine

D 957, No. 13. Original key: B minor. This is one of six Heine poems which form part of *Schwanengesang*. See "Der Atlas" for notes on Heine. See "Liebesbotschaft" for notes on *Schwanengesang*.

Der Doppelgänger	The Double
Still ist die Nacht, es ruhen die Gassen,	Still is the night; the streets are quiet.
In diesem Hause wohnte mein Schatz,	In this house lived my sweetheart.
Sie hat schon längst die Stadt verlassen,	She has long ago left the city,
Doch steht noch das Haus auf demselben Platz.	but the house still stands on the same site.
Da steht auch ein Mensch und starrt in die Höhe,	There stands also a man, and he is staring upwards
Und ringt die Hände vor Schmerzensgewalt;	and wringing his hands in anguish.
Mir graust es, wenn ich sein Antlitz sehe,	I shudder, when I see his face;
Der Mond zeigt mir meine eigne Gestalt.	the moon shows me my own self.
Du Doppelgänger, du bleicher Geselle,	You double, you pale companion,
Was äffst du nach mein Liebesleid,	why do you mimic the pain of my love
Das mich gequält auf dieser Stelle	which tormented me in this place
So manche Nacht, in alter Zeit?	so many a night, in old times?

sie hat schon längst_ die Stadt ver - las - sen, doch steht noch das

Haus_ auf dem-sel - ben Platz.

Da steht auch ein Mensch und starrt_ in die Hö - he, und ringt die

cresc. *poco a poco*

Hän - de vor Schmer - zens-ge-walt;_ mir_ graust es,

fff *ffz* *decresc.* *p*

Die Taubenpost

poem by Johann Gabriel Seidl

D 965 A, No. 14. Original key: G major. This song, Schubert's last, was composed in October of 1828 and premiered at a private recital on January 30, 1829, by Johann Michael Vogl. The publisher, Tobias Haslinger, added it to *Schwanengesang* for publication in May of 1829, but there is no indication that Schubert ever intended to include it with the Rellstab or Heine groupings. In measures 68 and 69 of the autograph, the word "die" is underlined for poetic emphasis. See "Die Männer sind méchant!" for notes on Seidl. See "Liebesbotschaft" for notes on *Schwanengesang*, and see "Ganymed" for notes on Vogl.

Die Taubenpost	The Pigeon Post
Ich hab eine Brieftaub in meinem Sold,	*I have a carrier-pigeon in my employment*
Die ist gar ergeben und treu;	*who is utterly loyal and true;*
Sie nimmt mir nie das Ziel zu kurz	*she never stops short of the goal for me,*
Und fliegt auch nie vorbei.	*and also never flies past it.*
Ich sende sie viel tausendmal	*I send her out many thousands of times*
Auf Kundschaft täglich hinaus,	*on daily reconnaissance,*
Vorbei an manchem lieben Ort,	*past many a beloved spot,*
Bis zu der Liebsten Haus.	*to my dearest beloved's house.*
Dort schaut sie zum Fenster heimlich hinein,	*There she gazes furtively into the window,*
Belauscht ihren Blick und Schritt,	*eavesdrops on her glance and step,*
Gibt meine Grüße scherzend ab	*delivers my greetings merrily,*
Und nimmt die ihren mit.	*and brings back hers.*
Kein Briefchen brauch ich zu schreiben mehr,	*No note need I write anymore;*
Die Träne selbst geb ich ihr,	*the tears themselves I give to her.*
Ah, sie verträgt sie sicher nicht,	*Ah, she will certainly not misplace them,*
Gar eifrig dient sie mir.	*so zealously does she serve me.*
Bei Tag, bei Nacht, im Wachen, im Traum,	*By day, by night, in waking, in dreaming,*
Ihr gilt das alles gleich,	*it is all the same to her;*
Wenn sie nur wandern, wandern kann,	*as long as she can roam,*
Dann ist sie überreich.	*then is she richly contented.*
Sie wird nicht müd, sie wird nicht matt,	*She does not get tired; she does not become weak.*
Der Weg ist stets ihr neu,	*The route is always new for her.*
Sie braucht nicht Lockung, braucht nicht Lohn,	*She needs not enticement, needs not reward,*
Die Taub ist so mir treu.	*so faithful is the pigeon to me.*
Drum heg ich sie auch so treu an der Brust,	*Therefore do I cherish her just as faithfully in my heart,*
Versichert des schönsten Gewinns;	*assured of the lovliest prize;*
Sie heißt: die Sehnsucht—kennt ihr sie?	*her name is "Longing"—do you know her?—*
Die Botin treuen Sinns.	*the messenger of fidelity.*

Ziemlich langsam

Ich hab ei-ne Brief-taub in mei-nem Sold, die ist gar er-ge-ben und treu; sie nimmt mir nie das Ziel zu kurz und fliegt auch nie vor-bei. Ich sen-de sie viel tau-send-mal auf Kund-schaft täg-lich hin-aus, vor-bei an man-chem

Ständchen

poem by William Shakespeare/August Wilhelm von Schlegel

D 889. Original key: C major. The text for this song, which is also known by the title, "Horch, horch! die Lerch," comes from Act II, Scene 3 of *Cymbeline*. Schubert used the Vienna *Shakespeare-Ausgabe* of 1825 as his source, and wrote the song while on a visit to Währing with Franz Schober. The autograph is dated July, 1826, and the song was published in October of 1830, in Book 7 of *Nachlass* (See "Abendstern"). Schlegel (1767–1845) was a poet, critic and philosopher. Brother to Friederich, he grew up in a literary household and studied at Göttingen before embarking on a career as a private tutor. He and his brother founded the literary journal *Das Athenaeum*, in 1798, and he became known as a leading exponent of Romantic ideas. In later life he devoted himself to the study of oriental languages. Schlegel's real legacy, his translation of seventeen of Shakespeare's plays into verse, contributed to Shakespeare's great popularity in Germany. See "An die Musik" for notes on Schober. See "Im Walde" for notes on Schlegel's brother.

Ständchen	*Serenade*
Horch, horch, die Lerch im Ätherblau,	*Hark, hark the lark in the blue sky;*
Und Phöbus, neu erweckt,	*and Phoebus, newly awakened,*
Tränkt seine Rosse mit dem Tau,	*waters his horses with the dew*
Der Blumenkelche deckt;	*that bedecks the flowers' chalices;*
Der Ringelblume Knospe schleußt	*the marigold bud opens*
Die goldnen Äuglein auf;	*its little golden eyes;*
Mit allem, was da reizend ist,	*with everything here which is charming,*
Du süße Maid, steh auf!	*you sweet maiden, arise!*

442

Sehnsucht

poem by Johann Gabriel Seidl

D 879. Original key: D minor. Seidl's poem was published in 1826, in a collection entitled *Lieder der Nacht* [Songs of the Night]. Schubert's manuscript of this song included two additional songs by Seidl and one by Franz Schlechta; the first page of the manuscript is dated March, 1826. "Sehnsucht" was published with three other Seidl songs as Opus 105, No. 4, by Josef Czerny, in November of 1828. Schubert wrote four other songs with the title "Sehnsucht," and set to poetry of Goethe (D 123), Mayrhofer (D 516), and Schiller (D 52 and D 636, using the same text). The earliest of these songs dates from April of 1813; this is his last. See "Die Männer sind méchant!" for notes on Seidl.

Sehnsucht

Die Scheibe friert, der Wind ist rauh,
Der nächt'ge Himmel rein und blau:
Ich sitz in meinem Kämmerlein
Und schau ins reine Blau hinein.

Mir fehlt etwas, das fühl ich gut,
Mir fehlt mein Lieb, das treue Blut:
Und will ich in die Sterne sehn,
Muss stets das Aug mir übergehn.

Mein Lieb, wo weilst du nur so fern,
Mein schöner Stern, mein Augenstern?
Du weißt, dich lieb und brauch ich ja,
Die Träne tritt mir wieder nah.

Da quält' ich mich so manchen Tag,
Weil mir kein Lied gelingen mag,—
Weil's nimmer sich erzwingen lässt
Und frei hinsäuselt wie der West.

Wie mild mich's wieder grad durchglüht—
Sieh nur—das ist ja schon ein Lied!
Wenn mich mein Los vom Liebchen warf,
Dann fühl ich, dass ich singen darf.

Longing

The window pane freezes, the wind is rough,
the night heaven clear and blue;
I sit in my little room
and gaze out into the clear blue.

I miss something, that I feel only too well;
I miss my dear one, my true love;
And when I look at the stars,
my eyes can't help constantly filling with tears.

My love, where tarry you so distant,
my beautiful star, my darling?
You know I love you and I need you so.
The tears are welling up again.

Thus have I agonized so many a day,
because I have not been able to succeed with any song—
because it never allows itself to be forced
and freely whispered forth, like the west wind.

How gently it warms through me again—
look now—that is indeed a song!
Though my fate cast me from my sweetheart,
still I feel that I can sing.

Sei mir gegrüßt

poem by Friedrich Rückert

D 741. Original key: B-flat major. Rückert's poem is a *ghazal*, an oriental verse form in which the verses are dominated by a single rhyme or phrase (See "Du liebst mich nicht"), and comes from his collection, *Östliche Rosen* [Oriental Roses]. The song, composed in 1822, is part of Opus 20, published by Sauer and Leidesdorf in April of 1823, and dedicated to Justine von Bruchmann, sister of Franz Bruchmann. "Sei mir gegrüßt" provided the theme for the third movement variations of Schubert's *Fantasy in C Major for Piano and Violin*, Opus 159, written in December of 1827. See "Daß sie hier gewesen!" for notes on Rückert. See "Am See" for notes on Bruchmann.

Sei mir gegrüßt	*I Greet You*
O du Entrissne mir und meinem Kusse;	*Oh you, torn from me and my kisses:*
Sei mir gegrüßt,	*I greet you,*
Sei mir geküsst.	*I kiss you.*
Erreichbar nur meinem Sehnsuchtsgruße;	*Attainable only by my yearning greeting,*
Sei mir gegrüßt,	*I greet you,*
Sei mir geküsst.	*I kiss you.*
Du, von der Hand der Liebe diesem Herzen	*You, by the hand of love to this heart*
Gegebne, du,	*given—you,*
Von dieser Brust	*from this breast*
Genommne mir! mit diesem Tränengusse	*taken from me! With this flood of tears*
Sei mir gegrüßt,	*I greet you,*
Sei mir geküsst.	*I kiss you.*
Zum Trotz der Ferne, die sich feindlich trennend	*Despite the distance which, hostilely divisive,*
Hat zwischen mich	*has between me*
Und dich gestellt,	*and you been placed,*
Dem Neid der Schicksalsmächte zum Verdrusse	*to the envy of the powers of fate, in spite,*
Sei mir gegrüßt,	*I greet you,*
Sei mir geküsst.	*I kiss you.*
Wie du mir je im schönsten Lenz der Liebe	*As you once to me, in the beautiful spring of love*
Mit Gruß und Kuss	*with greetings and kisses*
Entgegen kamst,	*came,*
Mit meiner Seele glühendstem Ergusse	*with my soul's most fervent outpouring*
Sei mir gegrüßt,	*I greet you,*
Sei mir geküsst.	*I kiss you.*
Ein Hauch der Liebe tilget Räum und Zeiten,	*One breath of love obliterates space and time;*
Ich bin bei dir,	*I am with you,*
Du bist bei mir,	*you are with me.*
Ich halte dich in dieses Arms Umschlusse,	*I hold you in these arms' embrace.*
Sei mir gegrüßt,	*I greet you,*
Sei mir geküsst!	*I kiss you!*

454

Seligkeit

poem by Ludwig Christoph Heinrich Hölty

D 433. Original key: E major. The poem dates from 1773. The song was composed in May of 1816 but remained unpublished until 1895. Today it's a favorite encore. Schubert set 23 Hölty poems, all but one from 1815–1816. See "An den Mond" for notes on Hölty.

Seligkeit	Bliss
Freuden sonder Zahl	*Joys without number*
Blühn im Himmelssaal	*bloom in heaven's hall*
Engeln und Verklärten,	*for angels and transfigured ones,*
Wie die Väter lehrten.	*as our fathers taught.*
O da möcht ich sein,	*Oh, there should I like to be,*
Und mich ewig freun!	*and forever rejoice!*
Jedem lächelt traut	*Upon everyone smiles intimately*
Eine Himmelsbraut;	*a heavenly bride;*
Harf und Psalter klinget,	*harp and psalter sound,*
Und man tanzt und singet.	*and one dances and sings.*
O da möcht ich sein,	*Oh, there should I like to be,*
Und mich ewig freun!	*and forever rejoice!*
Lieber bleib ich hier,	*Rather will I stay here,*
Lächelt Laura mir	*if Laura smiles upon me*
Einen Blick, der saget,	*a glance which says*
Dass ich ausgeklaget.	*that I've been freed from complaining.*
Selig dann mit ihr,	*Blissful then with her*
Bleib ich ewig hier!	*will I remain forever here!*

Verklärung

poem by Alexander Pope/Johann Gottfried Herder

D 59. Original key: A minor. This song was written on May 4, 1813, when Schubert was only 16, and published in May of 1832, in Book 17 of *Nachlass* (See "Abendstern") The poem is a translation of Pope's "The Dying Christian to His Soul," published in 1730. Pope (1688-1744) was the greatest English poet and satirist of his time. In addition to his own writings he found time to translate both the *Iliad* and the *Odyssey*. Herder (1744–1803) was a well known translator and poet. He was also the translator for one of Schubert's last songs, "Eine altschottische Ballade," D 923.

Verklärung

Lebensfunke, vom Himmel erglüht,
Der sich loszuwinden müht,
Zitternd, kühn, vor Sehnen leidend,
Gern, und doch mit Schmerzen scheidend!
End', o end' den Kampf, Natur!
Sanft ins Leben
Aufwärts schweben,
Sanft hinschwinden, lass mich nur!

Horch, mir lispeln Geister zu:
»Schwesterseele, komm zur Ruh!«
Ziehet was mich sanft von hinnen,
Was ist's, was mir meine Sinne,
Mir den Hauch zu rauben droht?
Seele! sprich, ist das der Tod?

Die Welt entweicht, sie ist nicht mehr.
Engel-Einklang um mich her!
Ich schweb im Morgenrot.
Leiht, o leiht mir eure Schwingen,
Ihr Brüder, Geister, helft mir singen:
»O Grab, wo ist dein Sieg? wo ist dein Pfeil, o Tod?«

Transfiguration

Spark of life, by heaven kindled,
which toils to wrench itself loose,
quivering, brave, suffering from longing,
gladly, and yet with pain, departing!
End, oh end the struggle, Nature!
Gently into life
upwards soaring,
gently let me but pass away!

Listen, spirits whisper to me:
"Sister-soul, come to rest!"
Is something drawing me gently hence?
What is it, that which my senses,
my breath, threatens to steal?
Soul, speak! Is that death?

The world vanishes; it is no more.
Angel harmony all around me!
I float in the sunrise.
Lend, oh lend me your wings;
you brothers, spirits, help me sing:
"Oh grave, where is your victory? Where is your arrow, oh death?"

Ich schweb im Mor - gen-rot. Leiht, o leiht mir eu - re

Schwin - gen, ihr Brü - der, Geis - ter, helft mir, helft mir sin - gen:

Recit.

»O Grab, wo ist dein Sieg? wo ist dein Pfeil, o Tod?«

Wandrers Nachtlied I

poem by Johann Wolfgang von Goethe

D 224. Original key: G-flat major. The poem was published in 1780, in a religious periodical *Christliches Magazin*. Schubert's composition, dated July 5, 1815, was published by Cappi and Diabelli in May of 1821 as Opus 4, No. 3, and dedicated to Johann Pyrker. See "An den Mond" for notes on Goethe. See "Die Allmacht" for notes on Pyrker.

Wandrers Nachtlied	*Wanderer's Night Song*
Der du von dem Himmel bist,	*You who are from heaven,*
Alles Leid und Schmerzen stillst,	*who all suffering and pain assuage—*
Den, der doppelt elend ist,	*he who is doubly wretched*
Doppelt mit Entzückung füllst,	*you doubly fill with delight.*
Ach! ich bin des Treibens müde!	*Ah, I am tired of striving!*
Was soll all der Schmerz und Lust?	*Why all the pain and desire?*
Süßer Friede!	*Sweet peace,*
Komm, ach, komm in meine Brust!	*come, ah, come to my breast!*

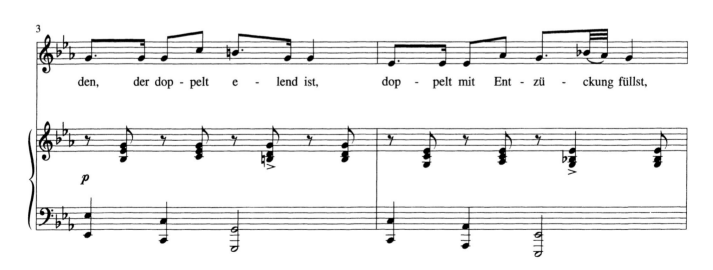

Wandrers Nachtlied II

poem by Johann Wolfgang von Goethe

D 768. Original key: B-flat major. In Goethe's collected works, this poem immediately follows "Wandrers Nachtlied I" and is titled "Ein Gleiches" [The Same]. Inspired by the stillness of the evening of September 6, 1780, Goethe wrote this poem on the wall of a hunter's blind outside the city of Ilmenau. Shortly before he died, Goethe returned to the blind to discover the now-faint lines still legible upon the wooden wall. The date of composition of the song is unknown, but it is believed that it was one of a group of Goethe settings composed in December of 1822. It was first published as a supplement to the *Zeitschrift für Kunst*, on June 23, 1827. Schober published it in 1828, as Opus 96, No. 3, with a dedication to the Princess von Kinsky. It was reprinted later that year by Probst of Leipzig, incorrectly numbered Opus 101. The poem has been set for solo voice and a variety of ensembles by many composers, including Loewe, Schumann and Liszt. See "An den Mond" for notes on Goethe.

Wandrers Nachtlied	*Wanderer's Night Song*
Über allen Gipfeln	*Over all the mountaintops*
Ist Ruh,	*is repose.*
In allen Wipfeln	*In all the treetops*
Spürest du	*you perceive*
Kaum einen Hauch;	*scarcely a breath;*
Die Vöglein schweigen im Walde,	*the little birds are silent in the forest.*
Warte nur,	*Only wait;*
Balde ruhest du auch.	*soon you will rest too.*

Wohin?

poem by Wilhelm Müller

D 795, No. 2. Original key: G major. This is the second song of the cycle *Die schöne Müllerin*. See "Der Neugierige" for notes on Müller and *Die schöne Müllerin*.

Wohin?	Whither?
Ich hört' ein Bächlein rauschen	I heard a brooklet rushing
Wohl aus dem Felsenquell,	from its rocky source,
Hinab zum Tale rauschen	down into the valley rushing
So frisch und wunderhell.	so fresh and wondrously clear.
Ich weiß nicht, wie mir wurde,	I know not how it came to me,
Nicht, wer den Rat mir gab,	nor who gave me the suggestion;
Ich musste auch hinunter	I too had to go down,
Mit meinem Wanderstab.	with my walking stick.
Hinunter und immer weiter	Down and always farther,
Und immer dem Bache nach,	and always following the brook;
Und immer heller rauschte	and always more brightly rushed,
Und immer heller der Bach.	and always brighter, the brook.
Ist das denn meine Straße?	Is this, then, my pathway?
O Bächlein, sprich, wohin?	Oh brooklet, tell: "Whither?"
Du hast mit deinem Rauschen	You have, with your rushing,
Mir ganz berauscht den Sinn.	completely enchanted my senses.
Was sag ich denn vom Rauschen?	Why am I talking about rushing?
Das kann kein Rauschen sein.	That can no rushing be.
Es singen wohl die Nixen	The water sprites must be singing,
Tief unten ihren Reihn.	deep below, to their roundelay.
Lass singen, Gesell, lass rauschen,	Let them sing, companion; let yourself rush
Und wandre fröhlich nach,	and go merrily onward.
Es gehn ja Mühlenräder	Mill wheels are turning
In jedem klaren Bach.	in every clear brook.

Suleika I

poem by Marianne von Willemer/rev. Johann Wolfgang von Goethe

D 720. Original key: B minor. The poem was written in September of 1815, while Willemer and Goethe were romantically involved. "Suleika I," addressed to the east wind, was written as Willemer traveled eastward from Frankfurt to Heidelberg, where she was to spend some time in Goethe's company. ("Suleika II" was written on her return trip.) Schubert's first draft, titled, "Suleika I. Göthe," is dated March, 1821. Dedicated to Franz von Schober, it was published by Cappi and Diabelli in December of 1822, as Opus 14, No. 1. Willemer (1784–1860), a German actress whose early history is not known, was adopted by the family of J.J. Willemer when she was 16. In 1814, mere weeks before she married Willemer, she entered into a brief but impassioned relationship with Goethe. See "An den Mond" for notes on Goethe. See "An die Musik" for notes on Schober.

Suleika I	Zuleika I
Was bedeutet die Bewegung?	*What means the stirring?*
Bringt der Ost mir frohe Kunde?	*Does the east wind bring me glad news?*
Seiner Schwingen frische Regung	*Its wings' refreshing motion*
Kühlt des Herzens tiefe Wunde.	*cools the heart's deep wound.*
Kosend spielt er mit dem Staube,	*Caressingly it plays with the dust,*
Jagt ihn auf in leichten Wölkchen,	*chases it upward in light little clouds,*
Treibt zur sichern Rebenlaube	*and drives into the secure grapevines' foliage*
Der Insekten frohes Völkchen.	*the happy swarm of insects.*
Lindert sanft der Sonne Glühen,	*Gently it tempers the sun's burning,*
Kühlt auch mir die heißen Wangen,	*and cools, likewise, my hot cheeks.*
Küsst die Reben noch im Fliehen,	*Even as it speeds by it kisses the grapes*
Die auf Feld und Hügel prangen.	*that sparkle on field and hill.*
Und mir bringt sein leises Flüstern	*And to me its soft whispering brings*
Von dem Freunde tausend Grüße;	*a thousand greetings from my friend;*
Eh noch diese Hügel düstern,	*before these hills grow dark,*
Grüßen mich wohl tausend Küsse.	*a thousand kisses will surely greet me.*
Und so kannst du weiter ziehen,	*And so you can continue onward!*
Diene Freunden und Betrübten.	*Serve friends and afflicted ones!*
Dort, wo hohe Mauern glühen,	*There, where high walls glow,*
Dort find ich bald den Vielgeliebten.	*there shall I soon find my well-beloved one.*
Ach! die wahre Herzenskunde,	*Ah, the true tidings of the heart,*
Liebeshauch, erfrischtes Leben,	*love's breath, renewed life,*
Wird mir nur aus seinem Munde,	*will come to me only from his mouth,*
Kann mir nur sein Atem geben.	*can only his breath give to me.*

Und so kannst du weiter zie – hen, die – ne

Freun – den und Be – trüb – ten, und so kannst du wei – ter

zie – hen, die – ne Freun – den und Be – trüb – ten.

Dort, dort, wo ho – he Mau – ern

127
wird mir nur aus sei - nem Mun - de, kann mir nur sein A - tem ge - ben, sein A - tem

cresc.

f >

p

>

131
ge - ben. Ach! die

ppp >

>

>

>

135
wah - re — Her - zens - kun - de, Lie - bes - hauch, er - frisch - tes Le - ben,

>

>

>

>

>

>

>

>

139
kann mir nur sein A - tem ge - ben.

>

>

>

>